I Know You Hurt, But There's
NOTHING TO BANDAGE

I know you hurt, but there's NOTHING TO BANDAGE

by DONALD D. FISHER, M.D.

THE TOUCHSTONE PRESS
P.O. Box 81
Beaverton, Oregon 97005

Acknowledgements

I am grateful to the many patients who have been considerate and forgiving with me over the years as I committed every error — and more — that I have placed at the feet of my medical colleagues in the pages that follow.

Special thanks go to Mrs. Carole Van Arsdol, a delightful and talented typist, who can read a physician's handwriting with the skill of a bright-eyed pharmacist. She has been of immeasurable help.

And last, but far from least, thanks to Tom Worcester, who came as an editor and left as a friend.

SECOND PRINTING
I.S.B.N. 0-911518-49-5

Contents

Foreword

ˈI first met Don Fisher through a telephone call from Portland, Oregon. He called me at my home in Montana to tell me how excited he was about the results he was getting with his patients from having them read my first book, *I AIN'T MUCH, BABY, BUT I'M ALL I GOT.*

Don suggested to many of his patients on their first visit that they take my book home and read it and then come back. His patients often found that by making changes in the ways they handled problems and their lives, their symptoms improved or disappeared.

I had heard of a few doctors who prescribed my book before but never one who used it so systematically. On my next trip to the West Coast, I met Don and he told me he was working on this book. I encouraged him to continue because the problem of our minds making our bodies sick was so important. I never dreamed, though, that Don could write such a good book. Most doctors seem forced into a style of speaking and writing that is very detached and academic. Don's book is the exact opposite. Because his writing is so clear and lucid, the central point stands out like a beacon for all of us to see.

We want to believe our illnesses are some outside enemy that is attacking our body. We want to believe our doctor will give us something to fight this enemy so we can get our body back to normal.

The process of sickness and health, we see from Don's book, is exactly opposite from the way we want to believe. Sickness is not so much an enemy from outside as it is a breakdown in our internal defenses. Once the body's natural walls against sickness are broken down, then the invaders from outside can come in. But even worse, many of our sicknesses do not come from outside but are already in us waiting to flare up when our body's defenses are weakened. So here we are, our own worst enemies, and worst of all, more often than not our illnesses imaginary and there is nothing wrong with our body yet. Our aches and pains come completely from the tension and problems in our minds. When we clear our minds, the aches and pains disappear without any harm to the body.

When we see illness the way it really is rather than the way our childish fantasies want to see it, then there are many new insights we have into ourselves that help us get well faster and stay well.

We see that most of our illnesses can be the beginning of the healing process because they call our attention to the problem, the break in our defense line against illness or the problems that bring about our imaginary illnesses. Our illness is like a fire-alarm that helps us put out the fire, and then eliminates the faulty wiring problem that caused it. Or if it's a false alarm, there's no fire and we can go in search of what set off the false alarm.

We see, too, that both patient and doctor have a different relationship to the healing process than we had previously thought. We used to think of the patient and doctor as innocent bystanders as they doctored the sick body of the patient. But now we see that the patient's mind isn't separated from the body but is part of it. We see, even more, that the mind is often the root of the illness. So the patient has to participate in his own cure. And in the process he can become a whole person with more resistance to the diseases that lurk inside and outside for a break in the body's defenses.

The doctor, too, is involved in the healing process not as a dispenser of pills but as a whole person engaged with another whole person in improving the patient's health. But a doctor can't lead a patient to better health without the doctor's openness to himself and life that can enable him to benefit from his own experience. And the doctor can't help but continually benefit himself by continuing to grow as a whole person as he helps his patients.

This to me is the wisdom Don has gained and is passing on to you in this book. I feel that Don's book gives us hope because we see our illnesses aren't as hard to conquer as we thought. I can see how his years of medical practice have benefited him. I hope you and I as readers can get some of the same benefit.

I personally have seen that my health has continually improved over the fourteen years since my first heart attack. Those of you who have read my books know that the path for better health for me hasn't been an easy one or a quick one, but it has been a steady one. As I approach the age of 50 I find I can be exceptionally active. I can powder-ski at high altitude and go elk hunting with my friends. I need to use some moderation but it is a thrill to be able to be so active when my health was practically destroyed by the time I was 35.

The ideas and the thinking in this book are what made me better. When Don read my first book, his initial reaction was, "How did Jess, without any medical knowledge, write the book I was going to write?" As you read this book of Don's, you will see that he didn't write the same book but that we both came to a similar set of ideas by a very different path.

Jess Lair, Ph.D.

Introduction

Have you ever felt totally miserable with some ailment and gone to your doctor for help and after extensive testing and examination been told, "Relax, you check fine"? It's confusing, isn't it? Here you are hurting and feeling lousy and you're told there's nothing to worry about. Simply said, you're "hurting but there's nothing to bandage."

You walk out of the doctor's office empty handed and confused or, more often than not, with a prescription for tranquilizers and all the more confused.

"If nothing is wrong, why does my stomach hurt and bloat everytime I eat? Something is causing these agonizing headaches. What can a tranquilizer do for my colitis and cramps? I'm more tired when I get up in the morning than when I went to bed and he wants to make me more tranquil? He must think it's 'all in my head.' "

It all sounds frightfully familiar doesn't it? I know. I'm in the practice of medicine and I play a role in the scene daily and that's my purpose for writing this book.

This story is making the rounds in medical circles. "A famous religious leader was standing in a long line of people awaiting his turn to cross the fabled gate and be processed into heaven. After waiting some time, his patience gave out and he stormed to the head of the line. He identified himself and curtly stated that because of his stature on earth, he felt he should be promptly admitted without going through the routine processing. The gatekeeper advised him that there were no favors or preferential treatment in heaven. He would have to get in line and wait his turn with all the rest of the faithful ones. As he was dejectedly walking away to get back in line a shiny sports car pulled up and the driver and car were promptly flagged through with a pleasant nod from the keeper of the gate.

"Wait a minute," snapped the religious leader. "Who was that getting through so easy?"

"It's all right," the gatekeeper reassured him. "That's God. He likes to play doctor."

It's a reversal of an old theme. Doctors do play God. Some doctors do it for the obvious reason: there are worse places to be than on a pedestal. Most doctors play God because the public, you and I, demand it. A Broadway play never goes on for years playing to an empty house, it's the same with doctors. Few of us are playing to empty offices.

Let's forget about the doctors who play the role because they need it. That won't help you and me. Let's concentrate on the doctors playing God or miracle worker because you and I demand it — by ordering reserve seats in the doctor's office months in advance.

But first let's look at you and me and our demands on doctors. Why do we exalt them and place them in God-like roles? Because we're all walking around with incurable ailments that require the services of a miracle worker.

Incurable ailments? Such as? Such as headaches, fatigue, ulcers, colitis, skin rashes and dizziness, for starters. They may not sound so incurable but they are. Think about it for a minute. It's easy to confuse temporary relief with a cure. Doctors give temporary relief. Only you can work on the "cure."

Most physicians agree that between seventy and eighty percent of the patients who visit their offices suffer from emotional and stress-related illnesses. Surgeons tend to lean somewhat the other way. As one surgeon friend of mine said, "That's what I like about surgery. You have a definite plan and you act in a positive manner. You get something accomplished." Then another surgeon confided to me, "You know if it wasn't for people screwing themselves up, I'd be drawing unemployment." I have to agree with the latter philosophy.

I have one patient who has had his stomach ulcer operated on "in a positive manner" eight times and is now being prepared for his ninth surgical cure — and at a teaching medical institution. Sounds like more "needless" surgery doesn't it? Maybe even malpractice? It isn't. He can't keep food down because his stomach is obstructed and he's bleeding from a new ulcer site. How about some insight and help from psychology? He's been offered that and it wouldn't cost him a cent, but he's not "buying" that approach. He's looking for a cure that doesn't exist. He needs a miracle worker, some talented surgeon who can remove stress with a knife. The trouble is, he's going to run out of stomach before he runs into self-acceptance. There's not much left to bandage, whether he's hurting or not.

Most of us aren't much different. We're looking desperately for answers and cures that simply don't exist. Doctors have been more than hesitant to point this out. We're slow to tell the patient that we don't have a pill or a surgical procedure that will solve the problem. Climbing onto a pedestal is invigorating. Climbing down from one causes pain with each step.

Doctors are put in the position of a friend of mine, Jim, who runs a garden supply store. Customers continually ask him a question that used to irritate him. After buying a packet of vegetable seeds, the customer frequently asks: "Now how many rows of radishes will this packet of seeds plant?" Jim used to say, "I really don't know, that's up to you and how you plant your garden." Even though the question is absurd, the answer didn't handle it. "Yes, but, surely you must know about how many rows on the average it will plant?" He could only shrug his shoulders or make a wild guess. In desperation, he had to come up with an acceptable answer. Now, no matter what the vegetable is or the size of the packet he sells them, he gives one standard authoritative answer. "The packet of seeds will plant exactly three rows." Jim expected a bundle of complaints the first season he started it. Now he's laughing. All he gets is a kind of mysterious admiration. The customer always comes in with a smile and says "you were absolutely right" — or "you only missed it by six inches" — "you really know your gardening."

That's patients and doctors. We all like to think someone else knows our "plot" better than we do. Doctors are driven to play the "pill packet" game. The results are about the same. If you and I are going to continue looking for answers that don't exist, we're going to get answers that do exist.

"Here, take this packet of pills. They should tranquilize you for exactly twenty-four hours a day." And they do. And isn't it a miracle?

You and I are going to have to start digging in our own gardens. We've got to decide what our "garden soul" is capable of and plant accordingly. How close can we plant the seeds? How full can we "cram" our days? How long should we make the rows? How far can we go without a day off or a vacation? How are we going to deal with the weeds? Is each one going to be a crisis in life's garden that requires a medical or alcoholic pesticide?

If we don't get control of our "life plot" then we'll have to fit our plot to the packet of pills much as Jim's customers do with their garden seed packet.

You and I, patients and doctors, can and must do better. Both parties are guilty. Patients are asking for the impossible and doctors are going to new technological limits to try and accommodate them. That's how doctors are trained. Every medical student is instructed to "first rule out organic disease." Rule out an X-Ray or laboratory-proven biological illness. Spare no expense. To me this medical school proverb suggests failure just the way it's worded. We're to rule things out. Shouldn't we be "ruling things in?"

Wouldn't it be more fitting to change the adage to "first rule in an emotional or stress related illness" since that's what the odds tell us the patient has? If we continue to look for biological causes that don't exist, we're going to have a lot of patients who don't feel good; who have an expensive collection of normal tests; who are "up" on tranquilizers and down on doctors. That pretty well describes what you and I see around us.

Patients are desperate and a massive wave of "self-care" is beginning to form in this country because of it. Some doctors feel threatened by this movement but I'm all for it. Self-care is bound to lead to self-prevention which will lead to self-acceptance which is the ultimate health goal, and that's what the book is about.

It's equally important to briefly state what the book is not. It's not about who's "right or wrong." I see enough of this. Like the gatekeeper in our story, no one, doctors nor patients, get preferential treatment. If I seem to fail in parts you'll have to read between the lines. It's there. It's not a book of answers to all your problems. You and I have those within us once we begin to identify our individual and varied problems. It's not a home medical advisor for self-care at home. But that's where the caring has to start and that's where our story begins.

My hope in writing this book is that you and I might discover the greatest physician in the world — ourselves. As one patient of long suffering said:

"I am in the conclusion of this chapter of my life, the first 38 years. The end can only be written with the passage of time, but my consolation is in the discovery of my problems because now I know what to do to correct them. And, that action will save my life."

Lake Oswego, Ore.   Donald D. Fisher, M.D.
January, 1978

1 – Only You Can Make It Better

My first physical this morning was Mary, a 48-year-old lady with 4 children – 3 boys in their teens and one girl, age 12.

"Doctor, I can't cope. I just can't cope. Excuse my tears – I'm sorry – I'd run away, I would – but there's no place to go. I'm sick, sick of it all. Last night the boys told me if they could ever choose parents again they certainly wouldn't choose us. I told them I had done the best I could and they said it wasn't good enough."

Mary cried herself through a long list of symptoms and ailments that she and I both knew were very real to her but were without organic cause. Repeated examinations and laboratory tests had all been normal. In spite of examinations and treatment and reassurances the symptoms have gradually become more painful, disabling, and threatening. We have treated, talked, tranquilized – tried this and that, but our poor results are very evident before us today. Mary has a long list of complaints written down. Severe headaches that won't stop, fatigue, dizziness, stomach cramps, shaky, heart pounding, easy to tears. She's not imagining them – they're very real. We do another complete examination and do all the usual laboratory tests and X-ray examination and what do we find? Nothing. Nothing to bandage!

Mary has heard this before and it doesn't help to hear it again. We've talked about changing some things in Mary's approach to life for the past sixteen years.

"I've tried, God knows I've tried, Doctor. This is living hell – I wish I had never been born. How can I do things to change the way I feel all the time? I can't remember feeling good. (More tears.) My biggest job is to try to keep from crying."

Mary is miserable and trapped by life itself. She is as sick as sick can be. Mary has found out that society and our immediate environment reinforce us not to change. In other words – we're expected not to change – don't make waves! She has an illness that no test will diagnose and no pill will cure. She has made herself ill and only she can make herself well.

Is Mary's case unusual? No. Seventy-five percent of all the patients I see have literally caused their own illnesses! Is this just my practice? Not at all! Every study and investigation that has been done on office practice patterns confirms this fact very clearly. If we need any other evidence, what medication is prescribed far and away above all others? Tranquilizers. They are the leading prescription drug sold in this country by far – even over antibiotics. Tranquilizers are prescribed so often that the Federal Drug Administration is rightfully concerned. The figures

11

may vary a bit, but all studies show that between sixty and eighty percent of office visits are for self-inflicted illnesses. To put this another way, seven out of the next ten visits you make to see your doctor will be for an illness that you caused yourself.

I always get strange looks when I am talking to a group and tell them this fact. Then I get a few questions about all those "other" funny people that make themselves ill — and what kind of a doctor am I anyway if my practice is mostly patients that are imagining that they're sick. I'm quick to tell them that I am not a psychoanalyst or psychiatrist — that I am in general practice, seeing patients just like them. I'm also very quick to tell them that all these patients are not imagining their ailments and that this is a crucial point. The tension headache caused by tight neck and scalp muscles is real — it really hurts. The pain from the irritable stomach or ulcer is very real — as is the gas and cramps associated with it. The asthma, the migraine headache, the colitis and diarrhea, the nervous skin rash with its intense itching — these and many other ailments are very real. It is the fact that they are so real that brings the patient to my office seeking relief. This is extremely important to make clear to the patient or we get nowhere. None of us wants to be told that our migraine headache that is pounding away was caused by the way we screwed up our day or week, or that we should take the day off and imagine it away. We want relief and we want it now — and that's the way it should be.

Sooner or later, however, if we're going to get well — and stay well — we're going to have to take a look at the illnesses that we are causing ourselves to suffer. This is where the going invariably gets a little bumpy, to say the least! Despite my efforts to explain this to the patient — that I know they hurt — that their symptoms are real and not imagined, many of them leave confused. What is so confusing is: "How can a calm, cool character like me be hurting this badly and have some doctor tell me that tension or stress is causing it?"

At this point the whole message gets lost. All too often the patient walks out the door, climbs in the car and when a husband or wife says, "Well — what did he say?" The reply is, "It's all in my head." Silence prevails and a doctor shopping spree begins. No one is going to lay out good money to be told, "It's all in your head." Right?

The patient is determined to find a doctor who, sooner or later, will stamp an organic label on the malady and treat it forever. Unfortunately, the patient doesn't usually have to shop too long. The words "tension" or "stress" will never be mentioned — after all, that's why the patient is here — he couldn't buy that tension and emotional bit. Plenty of fancy labels are available to cover any stress or emotional related illnesses. One of the more

12

popular current labels is hypoglycemia. Everyone suddenly has hypoglycemia — tiredness, weakness, headaches, anxiety, hunger, palpitations, sweating, and afternoon or evening mental weariness. Are there any symptoms here that you and I don't have all too often? And wouldn't it be comforting to have an "organic" cause for it — instead of being told we caused it with a lousy day? One of the leading authorities in medicine recently called hypoglycemia the most abused diagnosis in the United States — a fad, pure and simple.

Now, the doctor that finds a label for the patient may be well-meaning and sincere or he may be just a sincere quack. His quackery may be fairly obvious or it may be marginal and concealed under a host of different diplomas and certifications. Both types of quacks exist and in equal profusion. The more dangerous one I'm sure is the one that is well certified, whose praises are loudly sung by devoted (but among the newly poor) patients. The doctor, if he is sincere, has his back right against the wall. The patient begins by listing all his troubles, "I'm tired, I can't sleep, I have horrible headaches, I'm dizzy, gaining weight, and my heart pounds. And, I know it's not in my head — I've been told that before. Either you find out what's wrong, or else!"

At this point the doctor has to take a stand and he's got to come down hard. He's got to make a choice — and it can't be a little of this and a little of that — it won't do. It's like being a little bit pregnant. The doctor has one of two choices. He can become a hero (temporarily) by saying, "My God — you've got far advanced ity-bity-itis (a non-fatal expensive disease) and those other doctors called it 'nerves'? (Eyebrows cocked.) Thank goodness you found me before it was too late." Or, the doctor can look at his watch, glance out at the full waiting room and try in the time he doesn't have to try and gain insight into the tension and emotional factors that he knows are the basis of the problem. This is no fun — remember the patient knows it isn't in his head. So all too often the patient hears what he or she wants to hear — gets a handful of prescriptions, a pat on the back, and told to return regularly for the rest of his life. The patient walks proudly out with his chest held high and a "damn-those-other-doctors-anyway" attitude. When the patient gets home and reads up on the new "disease" that he has been christened with, he says: "Sure enough, those are my symptoms." And, the case is closed.

The trouble is the patient often looks up the wrong illness. If he looked up depression or anxiety or stress instead of the new label, he'd probably find the very same set of symptoms. Look back at the symptoms I listed for hypoglycemia. Every one of them can be caused by emotions. I'm not picking on hypoglycemia — I think it does exist. But, so does leprosy. I don't blame the patient. The benefits of having an illness of social acceptance are much greater than having an "illness of nerves." Try it — tell your friends you're having symptoms caused by tension and watch that look of "so what's new" spread over their faces. But tell them you have an illness with an organic label and you'll be run over by a mob of flower-bearers.

I have one patient (or I should say I had) Charlene, age 30, who I'd seen with headaches over a two-year period. I had examined her completely and did all the usual laboratory tests and evaluations and could find no organic cause. I sent her to two different neurologists who did extensive workups with numerous neurological tests. They also could find no organic cause for her headaches and she was sent back to me. I proposed trying to find the source of her tension and making some changes but she didn't keep her next appointment and I lost track of her. About a year later she saw me in the parking lot and came running up with a smile from ear to ear.

"Doctor, remember those headaches I was having? Well, they're completely gone!"

"Great," I said, waiting for the punch line. "How did you do it?"

"Well, I saw a Dr. Priley, a chiropractor, and he didn't waste any time. He took one look at me and said, 'You've got headaches haven't you?' Just like that. I hadn't even told him what I was in for — only his nurse knew. Then he told me I had a severe sinus condition that was causing all my trouble. He treated me with adjustments and I haven't had a headache since."

All I could say was "wonderful — just wonderful." I felt like the captain of the Titanic. Two neurologists and I had spent two years and much of her money and had not been of any concrete help and this guy walks in and with a snap of his fingers cures her. Besides hurting my poor tattered ego this got me to thinking. Why? What's going on here? What's the underlying principle? It's fairly obvious. The chiropractor sat in a very privileged position. He was aware that she had been seen and evaluated by several physicians and had been tested for everything possible. He knew that nothing had been found or she wouldn't be looking for help elsewhere. In other words, the diagnosis had already been made — there was nothing to bandage. All he had to do was apply his charm and put a label on her (one that had nothing to do with tension and all that messy stuff) and hesto-presto, a cure is forthcoming. I was wounded — to be sure, but I was also equally happy that Charlene was free of her miserable headaches. I thought to myself: "Why wasn't I smart enough to send her there in the first place? It would have solved the whole blasted problem (and saved my ego)." Or would it? Of course not. Why? Very simply — the stage had to be set first and the two neurologists and I set it with all the necessary props. We spent two years testing for every possible organic cause known to man and found none. All the time Charlene is saying, "My God — this must be something terrible — I've got 3 doctors scratching their heads?" This doesn't help the headaches. In fact, if they're based on tension they're going to be a lot worse at the end of two years which is bad enough. But then to be told: "There's no organic cause — it's no doubt tension." That's the final curtain call. Remember — Charlene's interpretation is, "It's all in my head." Charlene rejected this diagnosis 100 percent. After having family and friends worried for two years about what strange disease is incapacitating her, — Charlene can't go home and say, "It's only tension." Sinusitis may not be dramatic but the benefits sure outweigh being called a "neurotic."

Charlene will develop more symptoms over the years, but a quickie diagnosis won't work for the chiropractor next time because the stage won't be set. The tragic part is that Charlene will repeat the entire process over and over unless she begins to look at herself. The chances of this happening are not good in the future. After all, she just proved that three "so-called reputable" doctors were completely off base calling her headaches emotional or psychosomatic. Charlene will waste a good part of her life walking further and further down a symptom-strewn path, collecting social status benefits wherever she may, because of her "condition."

Charlene's story really doesn't end here because her children will very likely develop similar symptoms and tell their doctors: "Yes, my mother had them — I guess I inherited them." Do they really *inherit* anything? If your parents spoke English you'll probably speak English. But, you don't inherit it: you learn it and you're not even aware of it. It's like throwing a stone in a pond — the ripples spread on forever.

How have I arrived at these conclusions? How can I predict that Charlene and Mary will continue to lead unhappy lives filled with symptoms and labels — unless they make some drastic changes? Twenty years of practice and over 100,000 patient contacts have literally "told me so." It's an insight that can only be obtained by hearing what people have been saying from the deepest recesses of their hearts. This my patients have done, over and over again. That is why this book really is their story — not mine. My job has been to present their story, not to write it, and to hope that you and I can learn from it.

What can we do about preventing 70 percent of our illnesses? The first thing to do is to ask, "Could I be making myself sick?" This takes a lot of courage. No one wants to stand in front of the mirror and say, "Am I causing my problems?" But it's a basic First Step. Carl Rogers, a leading psychologist, said: "Once I accept my-self — then I can change." Sounds confusing, but think about it. Once I realize that I am mismanaging my day so badly that it is affecting my health — once I accept this — then I can change. The key word is accept. This doesn't mean approve or enjoy. All it says is accept. In other words, diagnose the situation. Then I can change. It doesn't mean that I will or that I have to change. It just means the path is open. Then it's up to you and me to change some things. Why is it so hard to get out of our ruts?

I think it's like the muddy road we used to ride on our bicycles as children. If we would follow some car tracks, the mud was packed and it was easier to pedal. It was less work to stay in the rut than pedal in the mud beside it. This works fine until the rut gets a little deeper. It's still easier to pedal but it's harder to turn the handlebars without wrecking ourself, because the rut is too deep. If we follow it far enough, it gets impossible to turn out of it because the sides of the rut grab the wheel and we lose control. At this point we can give one last twist on the handlebars and with a burst of speed try to break out, and we will no doubt end up with our head stuck in the mud — a disaster. Or we can put our feet out and plod on in until we're hopelessly mired down. This is about what happens with our go at life. We keep slogging down the same old rut until it takes a disaster to jolt us back to our senses. Oh, we may wiggle the handlebars once in a while to convince ourselves we've tried, but we really don't make many changes until tragedy hits. This can be a coronary, a bleeding ulcer, a stroke or just such a miserable existence that something has to be done. Many people can change after the disaster strikes. But how sad that it takes a major life threatening illness many times to get us out of our rut. Wouldn't it be nice if we could twist the handlebars, change our life patterns before the rut got so deep as to guarantee us a disaster?

We can!

Where can we go for help? Where can we learn some tricks? How can we spot that rut of least resistance but with the potential disaster waiting for us?

We can't all get help from formal psychiatry, for several reasons. First of all — there aren't enough psychiatrists to go around (depressing, isn't it?). Of more significance, the psychologist or psychiatrist sees the patient at the end of the trail. Everyone else has given up. The golden opportunity to change was years ago, when we were just entering the rut. The poor psychiatrist sees the patient after he has been in the rut so long he's nearly buried in dried mud. Then the patient and the psychiatrist spend months trying to find out what mother did wrong that made the rut seem so attractive in the first place. Meanwhile they begin picking the mud off with a toothpick. The first two years are spent explaining to you, the patient, all the reasons you have for being so mixed up and the next ten are spent showing you how dependent you are on the psychiatrist if you're going to be able to live with your new label — paranoid, depressive, passive, aggressive, impulse ridden, neurotic, schizophrenic or whatever. Look at the endless list of psychiatric disorders in the *American Psychiatric Association Diagnostic Manual*. It's enough to give anyone a withdrawal reaction. The patient doesn't "have an illness" — he "becomes a condition." It's all programmed out for him.

I think we're bogged down with long labels that don't really help. The patient is shown what all he's entitled to with his new diagnosis and long term therapy that all too often leads nowhere. It's a bit like kissing your sister. I personally know of one patient who has been getting psychiatric help once a week for the past 34 years.

To me, this seems like taking my car to the mechanic for repairs and having him tell me what's wrong — and then asking me to explain how I've driven it each day for the past 10 years. What I really need is to get the car fixed. If it's my driving habits that are causing the trouble — I want to know and I'll try to correct it, but I don't want him to drive my car for the rest of my life. I'm sure I couldn't afford it and neither can the rest of you. If he offered to, I'm sure I would pose at least two good questions. Where are we going and when can we expect to arrive?

I am not personally down on psychiatry. In the future, the main emphasis in medicine will have to be in this area, as perhaps is demonstrated by an unpublished report by the National Committee on Mental Health. The committee feels that the problem of emotional and mental illnesses in this country is far greater than they had suspected originally. Committee members feel that all doctors in primary care are going to have to assume more responsibility in this area. Their figures show that the number of psychiatrists and psychologists in the country is desperately short of the need.

Not only do we need more help, but we need some new approaches that are more effective, less time consuming and less expensive. A standardization of terms and what they mean would be a start. I've been through too many erudite psychological conferences where I had the distinct feeling no one knew what the other person was saying, or why, but dared not ask for fear of appearing stupid. The newspaper account of any publicized criminal trial leaves most of us confused. The psychological testimony for and against the defendant is enough to confuse the judge, the jury, the reader and possibly even the defendant. I know it is the attorney's duty to try to confuse the jury with conflicting testimony, but I feel both attorneys could take the day off when a few opposing psychological experts are on the witness stand. Everyone will be confused enough!

We need to shore up our psychological theories with some

solid scientific foundations. We're spending too much time trying to understand what Freud meant years ago and how we can apply his thoughts. Our aviation technology would be in a similar stage if instead of developing modern aircraft, aeronautical engineers had spent the last 50 years crawling over the Wright Brothers' airplane trying to analyze what the brothers had in mind.

Too many of my patients come in and tell me: "You see, doctor, there's something you should know — I've been diagnosed as a 'manic depressive' or 'obsessive compulsive' or 'neurotic.'" It's like a badge they wear. They feel they have to perform in a certain arena with this label on it, and I should understand. I don't even use these terms. In fact, I think we should close up the label shop. We really ought to be changing some daily patterns, not finding a psychiatric label that justifies continuing the old ones.

The most likely source of help should be the physician that you see when you develop symptoms. He's going to be the first professional you talk to about your illness. It's going to be up to him to decide, with your help, whether tension and stress are at the bottom of the problems. Remember the odds — 70 percent of the time it's a stress-related illness. So, if it isn't related to stress — we better question it.

Now the real distressing thing to me is that most physicians are fully aware of this data but do not follow through. Most physicians have a full waiting room and patients are allotted about 15 minutes each. It's a lot easier to do a few tests and put a label on the symptoms than to ask what's really behind all this. This is why we treat the same stomach or bowel problem forever. We see the same patient coming in two or three times a year with an "irritable bowel" or stomach problem year after year. If it goes on long enough, we come to surgery. After surgery the problem can start all over. As I said, I have one patient who has had eight operations for ulcers, and is being prepared for the ninth operation. How absurd! Think of all your friends who have had stomach troubles or a colitis — or an "irritable bowel." It isn't the bowel that's irritated — it's the mind. Or, as I say, it's not the bowel, it's the growl.

If your physician doesn't bring up emotional factors, bring them up yourself. He may be uncomfortable about it or too busy, but it's your health. If he's not tuned in this way, find one who is!

I recently attended a conference on stomach and colon disorders. One speaker of national prominence discussed the cause behind most bowel disorders. He felt they could be listed as infectious, auto immune or psychological. Then he said, "The psychological theories can pretty well be 'shot down.'" This bothered me a lot and I cornered him after the lecture. I asked him what percentage of all of his colon cases did he feel were on an emotional basis. He paused for a second and said, "At least 75 percent." I asked him why he tended to throw it out of his discussion and he said, "Because treating emotional factors is so time consuming, it's not practical!"

If we can't get the help we need from the physician, where *do* we turn? It's been very embarrassing to me on a few occasions to try to treat a patient both for the emotional problem and his physical symptom and get nowhere. Then one day the patient comes in looking like a different soul entirely and completely on top of the problem. When I ask what happened I'm usually surprised to hear them say, "Well, one of my friends recommended this book and it's just been great! I've gotten more out of the book and feel better than I did with all the pills I was on." This may be hard on my ego, but it's blessed for the patient. This is a real source of help that most physicians have overlooked. Perhaps the reason is that the patient can spend hours with a book in his spare time. The attitude while reading is entirely different. In the doctor's office, the patient is nervous, being probed here and there and more or less on the pan. I'm not embarrassed anymore because I now recommend more books than pills. The patient and I can save hours by having him do his own homework.

There are hundreds of books out on emotions and self-improvement. Walk into the bookstore and look under the "psychology sections." That alone testifies to the increase in stress and unhappiness in the 20th Century at least in the eyes of the publishers. It's also interesting to note that one or two of these are always on the best selling list.

With all those books, where do we start? The ones that have helped my patients the most are *Psychocybernetics*, by Dr. Maxwell Maltz, *I'm OK — You're OK*, by Dr. Thomas A. Harris and *I Ain't Much, Baby, But I'm All I've Got*, by Dr. Jess Lair. All provide excellent recipes for better living. You can't read them once and give them to "someone who really needs it." You've got to see yourself on every page and say, "Yep, that's me. I'll work on that!" These authors are talking to you — not your wife or children or friends.

I've seen these books change lives in a manner I didn't think was possible. I'm now totally convinced that anyone can change into the type of person he wants to be. I'm also totally convinced that no one wants to be miserable. If we are — we're just feeding the wrong material into our poor old computer.

One of my favorite Christmas cards each year comes from Helen and her family of 7. They usually have a family portrait on the card and I get a glow on just looking at it.

Helen literally owes her health, her sanity and the past several years of fun-packed times to Dr. Maltz's book, *Psychocybernetics.* Helen was the most miserable 31-year-old gal I had ever seen. I treated her and we got absolutely nowhere. She had everything wrong with her that one could possible imagine. She had so many symptoms that I could hardly get them recorded, much less treated. The office help ran when they saw her come in and alerted me that "she" was here. She was arrogant, aloof, picky, complaining. In short, totally obnoxious.

Her real problem was that she was in the midst of a 12-year-old marriage that had been a nightmare since day one. Helen's husband was a foul-talking, foul-acting, sadist in private and a perfect gentleman in public. In most marriages, the score sheet is about even but in Helen's case it wasn't. She and the three children had honestly and sincerely tried to the best of their ability. Helen's parents and all of her friends thought she should stick it out. So Helen not only had her own thoughts of, "Maybe it's me, maybe he'll change, I've got to stick it out for the kids." She had to live up to the expectations of her mother and her friends. Helen reacted by lashing out at the world and her children. What would you and I do? After one especially foul and sadistic encounter Helen had had it. She read *Psychocybernetics* and devoured every page. Later on she obtained a divorce. These two factors literally changed Helen's life. She applied what she had read. She did not become a bitter divorcee with a chip on her shoulder which can easily happen. Helen changed in an unbelievable manner. The office girls became totally intrigued with her new behavior and asked me what new pills she was on and what things we were talking about. I couldn't take the credit. I had tried hard but I had really not helped her. Helen's case totally convinced me that anyone can dramatically change his life, regain his health and start a life of fun if only he will. Helen and her new family have had a ball these past 5 years. I had to ask myself, would the divorce alone have brought about the results? I doubt it when I look at so many divorces and see the usual pattern of relief, remorse and regret. Had Helen not gained a lot of insight into herself, I doubt that she would have found the new husband that she did.

Dr. Harris's book, *I'm OK — You're OK* has been a help to a considerable number of patients. The book shows us the roles that we're playing, how we are relating to others and how we are using our illnesses for all they're worth.

Dr. Jess Lair has written a classic in *I Ain't Much, Baby, But I'm All I've Got*. Dr. Lair had to learn the hard way. He had to have a coronary attack at age 35 to get him out of that muddy rut. He got out of a business that was killing him (literally) and ended up in psychology. He has written a book that will help thousands transform their lives if only they will read it and act on it.

One of my patients, a 33-year-old fellow had had 18-20 petit mal seizures (a small epileptiform seizure) every day of his life for as long as he could remember. He was a hard driver, had his own successful business, and had never talked to anyone about this, including his wife and family. Since the seizures are the type that are only a very short hesitancy of speech or a slight momentary stare, he felt he had been able to "get by with no one being aware of it." He noticed any form of pressure made them worse. I had him stop taking dilantin, the usual drug given for epilepsy, and placed him on valium. I asked him to read Dr. Lair's book and he came back in three weeks and had had only one seizure. He was absolutely amazed with himself. He couldn't believe it because he had never had a day free of them. He had changed his schedule, was getting a new look at things and had been giving himself five minutes a day to reflect. Nine months later he had had so few that, he said, "I can't even remember when I had the last one."

Another patient, a 62-year-old registered nurse, came to see me because she was having 20-30 severe episodes of anginal pain each month. These pains were so severe that they were beginning to disable her in her work. I assigned her Dr. Lair's book, *I Ain't Much, Baby, But I'm All I've Got*, and she studied it carefully. She began to reduce her angina and brought me a graphic record of her anginal attacks that she had been keeping from the beginning. One month after reading the book the anginal attacks were reduced to 19 attacks a month and then they fell off to 2-3 anginal attacks a month. When I last saw her she had had two anginal attacks in the last four months. She had changed her entire outlook. "I had to if I was going to live," she said. Her nursing and home situation had not changed, but her interpretation of them had. She now finds time for herself despite a busy nursing job, an elderly mother and a retired husband to care for. She looks like a different person — and she is!

At a recent symposium on death and dying one of the speakers said he helped a dying patient through the final day by telling him, "You have more control over your body than you have any idea of." After that the patient became more resigned and spent his last days in more comfort and required less sedation and pain medication.

I couldn't help but think as I listened, "What great advice, but why save it for the dying?" If it can help this much at the end of life, what could it do somewhere along the way? The fact that most of us don't take control of our bodies is attested to by the staggering sales of prescription tranquilizers and pain medications. We take over one hundred million aspirin every day in this country. And how many television commercials try to sell you something for the "storm in your stomach" or "the heartbreak of psoriasis." Let's say it right. The storm is in our head not our stomach, and we ought to call it "the psoriasis of heartbreak" if we're really putting things in perspective.

One gastroenterologist feels that ulcers, ulcerative colitis,

irritable colon and diverticulitis are diseases of "modern civiliza-
tion, and they're getting more common all the time." He also felt
that they have a pattern of "rhythmicity, periodicity and
chronicity." In other words, no one gets well. We just keep
messing up until we get another bout. The more bouts we have,
the more the body computer is programmed to set up another
round.

Ulcers have been called a "disease of dignity." As one doctor
said, "they're nothing to be ashamed of." Maybe this is what I
have to fight when I take an "upper GI" and tell the patient that
he has no ulcer. The patient usually looks dejected. Before I can
finish the patient will frequently ask, "Are you sure?"

I reassure him I'm sure and that that's good news.

"Well, I guess it's good news, but then what is it? I'm not
imagining the pain."

After explaining that your stomach can hurt and can still be
inflamed without an ulcer crater in it, the patient relaxes a bit.
He's sure, however, that tension or a nervous stomach couldn't
cause all that pain. I explain that if he wants an ulcer he'll have to
keep his tension and emotional conflict going for a bit longer and
then he'll have one. I repeat that it is "Good News!" He's lucky.
He's only on the road to an ulcer and that he and I can probably
prevent it proceeding to an ulcer. In spite of all this explanation, it
usually doesn't set too well. I usually hear, "I was afraid they (the
X-rays) wouldn't show anything." I've robbed him of his "disease
of dignity."

I recently had a 30-year-old man come in complaining of
"ulcer pain." "I'm sure I have one, doctor. I'm sure I've had one in
the past, but they've never been able to find it," he said. He
requested that I do an "upper GI." Upon examination, I found he
was quite tender over the stomach in the duodenal area and I felt
an upper GI was possibly warranted. I ordered one and the results
came back normal.

"That's hard to believe," he said. "I must at least have the
makings of one, don't I? My mother told me at age 8, that she
knew I was going to have an ulcer sooner or later. She told me that
every year that I was growing up and still tells me that everytime
she sees me. She's going to be disappointed," he sighed.

Isn't it sad, he's going to disappoint Mother because he
doesn't have an ulcer. It seems we all need "something to
bandage."

I had this need for a specific diagnosis carried to extreme two
years ago when a middle aged man came in with chest pain. He
was physically and emotionally drained. I studied him thoroughly
and was convinced that a heart attack was not in the offing. I told
him so. He looked at the floor, hands on his chin for a few
moments. Then he looked up and said, "Doctor, I was afraid

you'd say that. You won't understand, but I actually wish it was my heart." I understood. He was looking for any ray of hope. A heart attack would have helped immeasurably from his viewpoint. He wasn't considering that it might take his life any more than a potential suicide victim. It would have been a temporary (and possibly permanent) solution. He was crying for help in the only way he knew. A heart attack would have sent him to the hospital. It would stop the terrible strain he had been under at work, the tables would begin to turn. Now people would know that he was sick − really sick − the demands of work would stop immediately. He couldn't be expected to increase his sales quota next week and probably never. He knew the boss would say, "Fred, when you get out you're not going to put in such long hours, I'll see to that." He knew things would have to change after he had a heart attack and to Fred it was all worth it from his desperate vantage point.

Fred was lucky. We worked out some alternatives that have helped much more than a coronary attack would have and he looks back and laughs at himself four years ago. Four hundred and fifty thousand Americans each year aren't so lucky and have "sudden unsuspected cardiac deaths." At a post graduate cardiac seminar numerous factors were discussed as to why there were so many unexpected cardiac deaths. One noted cardiologist was asked what he thought we could do to prevent them.

His answer was profound.

"I feel a psychological adjustment of the patient would be the biggest help."

It was a short statement and rapidly got lost in the hours of discussion that followed about cardiac research, newer and more complicated testing, heart surgery, cardiac catheterization, etc. It wasn't mentioned again all day. "Psychological adjustment" − and this coming from a cardiologist, not a psychiatrist.

A major study of coronary heart disease has been underway in this country for 16 years called the "Framingham Study." Four major factors of sudden death were considered: elevated blood pressure, overweight, the cigarette habit and an enlarged left ventricle of the heart. Emotional stress was *conceded* to be a "significant factor" but was not included at all. Why? The investigators felt it was "not specific and was difficult to measure."

Emotional stress is significant, and maybe that explains why that even though doctors have cut down on their smoking, reduced their weight and cholesterol intake over the past 20 years, a recent study showed that we haven't altered the incidence of coronary attacks in doctors one bit. We're getting just as many heart attacks and at just as early an age as we did 20 years ago. Maybe we had better take another look at the emotional factors even though they are "hard to measure."

A small rural town, Surprise, Nebraska, has one of the outstanding longevity records in the United States. Many of the people in the community are in their 70s and 80s and they're mainly all retired farming people. What have these people been eating for the past 70 or 80 years? All the cream, butter, eggs and bacon that they could raise. They hadn't heard of cholestrol or triglycerides. They also didn't live in what Dr. Beverly Mead, a psychiatrist, calls the "hijacked screaming jet age."

Somehow it doesn't quite fit. That's why all the heated medical arguments over the entire cholesterol problem. The studies are inconclusive and have not proven that lowering cholesterol prolongs one's life. Actually, our bodies need some cholesterol to function. Cholesterol is an important chemical in our male and female sex hormones. That alone is enough to make some of us put three eggs in our morning cup of coffee! I think it's rather obvious that our bodies usually will handle the cholesterol if we don't raise it artificially with stress. We *can* do this and we do it all the time.

A study of prisoners who had volunteered for medical research demonstrates this fact. The prisoners were told that they were going down to the parole board and would no doubt get their parole. On the way down, each one stopped at the prison laboratory and had cholesterol levels drawn. Then they went to the parole meeting and were brusquely told that their parole was being denied. They were understandably furious and were taken back to the hospital laboratory where another cholesterol level was drawn. In a period of 20 minutes time, they had raised their cholesterol levels significantly.

How many times do we raise our cholesterol levels with stress? How many times do we constrict the arteries in our hearts when the going gets rough?

Consider what happens when you're good and mad, or insulted. Look at someone's face become flushed or pale under similar situations. How do we blush or become ashen pale? Easy — we just dilate or constrict the arteries in our face. Now we really don't plan all this — "face get red or pale — I'll show them." It's all done in a split second for us. It happens without our even thinking about it. You had no apparent control over the physical changes *once* you got angry or embarrassed. If this can happen in the face, how about the brain and maybe a headache or a little vertigo or dizziness? And, what about the heart with angina pectoris or an outright heart attack? How about the bowel with an irritable, inflamed colon? There is a fine point to make here. Once we've set the emotion in action the computer takes over and plays what we have programmed over the years. This is what it's all about.

If we can control the emotion, and we can, then we'll get the computer to send a different set of impulses along our subconscious nerve pathways. If we can't control our emotional factors, we can at least start working on it.

I was called to see a 33-year-old man who had just been brought to the hospital with a suspected heart attack. I had not seen him before and did not know his medical history. I saw him immediately and ordered an electrocardiogram. He was comfortable and while I awaited the cardiogram I examined him and talked to him briefly about his medical condition. He was very muscular and a picture of health. He told me he worked out daily (this was obvious) and avoided cholesterol rich foods. I asked him what he had been doing when the pain hit him and he said, "Nothing special — just driving to work."

"How about the day before?" I asked.

"About the same," he answered. "Nothing really unusual. Well, I take that back. We had a sales meeting last night and I got madder than I've ever been in my life." Right then he had another severe pain and despite resuscitation efforts died immediately. At autopsy his coronary arteries looked fine. The pathology report showed "no embolus (clot) and no significant arteriosclerosis of the coronary arteries." He didn't die with coronary artery disease, he died with "sales meeting heart disease." His death certificate should read, "death secondary to sales meeting anger resulting in coronary artery spasm." It would have had a lot more meaning and it would have come a lot closer to the real cause than just calling it a myocardial infarct. It's true that he died with a heart attack, that an area of the heart wall was damaged, but it was due strictly to spasm of the coronary artery and not a clot or embolism.

How many other death certificates should read "business heart disease, marriage heart disease, parent heart disease," etc? But, who would believe such silly sounding medical afflictions?

I believe in them and I hope that by the end of the book you will too, and can start taking steps on your own to avoid them.

Emerson said it so well in his lecture on "The Duties of a Scholar" in which he quotes the melancholy Pestalossi who said, "I have learned that no one in God's wide earth is either willing or able to help any other man." Emerson said, "Help must come from the bosom alone!"

2 – The Mental Wheelchair Syndrome

Recently an ad in a national magazine stated, "A mind is a terrible thing to waste." It depicted a young Negro boy in a ghetto setting looking pensive and forlorn. The message is well taken but it got me thinking. How about the body, how about an ad, "The body is a terrible thing to waste." Aren't we wasting as many bodies as minds, if not more. What if we develop our IQs beyond belief but destroy our bodies in the process. Maybe the whole thing is academic, but I think it's about time we started giving our poor old bodies equal billing. It may not be as headline grabbing but it certainly warrants equal consideration. I think the truth is we really can't separate the mind and the body too far anyway. If we try to do this one or the other, the mind or the body (or both) begin to suffer. The hard part of all this is that we have to try to do it right the first time around. We're not like the proverbial cat with nine lives. We've only got one chance to put it all together and unfortunately too many of us wake up too late, if ever. The longer we continue to do things wrong the more damage is done and the harder the whole mess is to correct. At one time I would have said impossible to correct but I won't buy this anymore. I've seen too many patients now who have shown me that they can change rather dramatically from symptom ridden downcast individuals into people who are symptom free and full of zest, even after years of physical and mental suffering. So it "CAN BE DONE."

Too often I've noticed the patient sees more benefits in being sick, of having a "condition," than being well. Sometimes this can be pretty well hidden and almost at the subconscious level, especially after years of wearing mental blinders. All too frequently it's right out in the open, the patient is perfectly aware of it and makes vigorous efforts to hold onto his or her illness. Sounds absurd? Let's take a closer look at some specifics.

How many of you have asked someone to do something with you or for you and have been told, "I'd love too, but you know I have such and such condition and I just can't." They almost have a twinkle in their voice and can't wait to lay it on you, and you probably heard it a year ago and forgot or you wouldn't have asked again.

Insurance companies and industry foster this in subtle ways. The patient comes in and states, "I have to be off sick at least four or eight (or some magical number) days or I won't get paid for my time off." If he is only off one or two days as needed, no deal. I've never understood why policies are written that way and I am sure there are millions of working days lost because of it. I'm not so much concerned about the lost days as I am about the seed that gets planted.

Numerous insurance ads claim to pay the patient some fifty dollars a day for every day that he is in the hospital. Conclusion — the longer you stay ill and in the hospital the better financial deal you've got. I even saw one ad that said, "You may be dollars ahead after your illness." If you look at some insurance policies it becomes obvious that it's a money losing proposition to start getting well. Watch the benefits drop when you are no longer bed or house confined or no longer have to be examined by the doctor once or twice a week. I don't think we're all a bunch of crooks, but we're also not stupid. These may be minor and subtle motivations to stay ill but I see them working all the time. I think the whole approach is wrong — we ought to be rewarding people to get well and stay well, not to bask in the spotlight of an illness. It's what I call the mental wheel chair syndrome and it drives most doctors to despair. As one colleague put it, "The problem isn't *getting* people well — it's convincing them that they *are* well."

But why call it the mental wheel chair syndrome? What about a wheel chair? It speaks for itself, doesn't it? The occupant deserves special help; he has a handicap for all the world to see. He has a problem that limits him by definition and it also limits what we can expect of him. The benefits become obvious. Let me state that the only ones who will never have the mental wheel chair syndrome are the ones in the actual wheel chair! They've got the real thing and they are invariably independent, self-sufficient, productive people. But there's an important difference here. The people in the real wheel chair didn't develop the wheel chair syndrome. They were forced into it by a physical tragedy of some sort.

Let me give you an example that portrays this problem. A middle aged lady came in stating that life was "living hell — I'd be better off to my family if I was dead." Arlene had a delightful pair of daughters and a devoted home loving husband. Her daughters were nearing the end of high school. Ten years before she had developed severe headaches and muscular spasm of her neck. She remembers the day that they came but she is unable to give any possible cause for their onset. "One day I was shopping and this funny feeling just hit me. I don't know why — I've thought and thought." Interestingly, Arlene has not sought much medical care for this. She saw a doctor originally who felt that it was probably on an emotional basis and recommended emotional care. She went for psychological counseling twice but, "we couldn't afford it." (The family is quite well off financially.)

Arlene relates, "I would give anything to be free of this. I haven't been able to drive the children anywhere all during their grade school years. I can't even drive to the grocery store. The neighbors have driven the children all this time and my husband takes me shopping in the evening and on weekends. I don't know how he does it. He's been so patient, but at times I think he resents it. He'd like to leave once in a while to fish and hunt on the weekend but he knows he shouldn't in case I should get worse. I don't even like to be with other people without him. Sometimes I wonder if he will continue to understand."

"Have you ever tried to drive since your original attack?" I asked.

"Oh no, I wouldn't dare, I just know I wouldn't make it. It's so terrible, doctor, you just can't appreciate the hell I'm going through."

Arlene just didn't look like she was enduring living hell. I asked her what she took for the pain. "Oh, an aspirin will usually relieve it," she said. She nearly smiled when she repeated the story. I did a complete examination and all of the tests and examinations were normal. Arlene wasn't concerned at all about the normal findings.

"I knew you wouldn't find anything," she said.

I suggested we set up some times to talk about this and see if we could get her back doing the things she would like to do. She kept one appointment and didn't show up for the next one. Why? "We can't afford it." I decided the challenge was too great. I had a strong feeling Arlene had no desire to change. I removed the final obstacle by saying, "Fine, I've got a deal you can't resist. We'll do this free of charge. I'll be glad to do it just to get you some help." She made and kept one more appointment and that was it.

Living hell? I doubt it. I think it was more like "heaven on earth." What's so bad about all this? How many women would love to get out of driving once in a while much less all the time. My wife felt like a veritable taxi driver for eight years while the girls were growing up.

Arlene has had her husband corralled continuously. His evenings and weekends were spent "attending" her. I know many wives who would love just a portion of this attention, even one night, even if they had to "nag" to get it. Arlene gets it and no one can even complain. After all, "her condition."

Does Arlene want out? Of course not. She proved this. I removed her last defense and she wouldn't even play the game. She had the mental wheel chair syndrome and she was not about to lose it. The benefits far outweighed the disadvantages. Arlene can't afford to "get well" and she won't unless she sees her situation for what it is. The sad part of it though is that she really can't completely enjoy it because it is a full time job keeping her face twisted with unmitigating pain that doesn't exist. She's almost got herself sick in the process. As someone once said, "It's bad enough to be sick without being miserable." It's equally bad, or worse, to be "miserable without being sick."

Insurance companies and industry aren't the only "bad guys" behind all this. Compared to doctors and attorneys they're hopeless amateurs at keeping people in mental wheel chairs. The insurance companies are really just the coin changers in the whole transaction.

The ridiculous aspect of their role is that they don't know what is going on. They have no idea of the number of mental wheel chair syndromes that they foster and pay for. (Who's paying?) Why? Because they assume emotional problems don't exist in this country. Why? Because all doctors tell them so on each insurance form they complete. Why? Because the insurance agent, the patient, the hospital and the doctor all know that the policy doesn't cover "emotional illnesses."

The solution is very simple: Don't call anything the way it is. But, isn't that fraud? Come now, would insurance agents, patients, hospital record clerks and of all people, *doctors,* commit fraud? You're right, of course not. After all, we're professionals, we can handle it a lot smoother than that. We just turn our head the other way.

For example, we have a patient whose mental wheel chair syndrome no longer works, who is battle weary with the unending social war, and who decides to end it all by leaping out of the fourth story window. Now if the poor soul dies the case is obvious. If he or she survives the fall and hospital care, we've got problems at the end of two weeks when the $4,000 or $5,000 bill comes due. Remember if it's emotional, it's "not covered," the insurance company won't pay. That's enough to make you pick the twelfth floor the next time you jump. So what does the final diagnosis on the hospital chart say?

I. 1. Multiple bruises (bleeding tendency on father's side)
    2. Numerous lacerations (secondary to sudden deceleration)
    3. Thirty-two teeth absent (history of pyorrhea and numerous sweets between meals as a child)
    4. Thirteen assorted fractures (gives history of poor eating habits and has an allergy to milk)
    5. Ruptured urinary bladder (had bed wetting problem as a child)
    6. Flower pot imbedded in right buttocks (patient is an avid gardener)
    7. Pneumonia (patient admits to being in a recent terrifying draft)
II. All or some of above directly or indirectly due to unsuccessful sky diving and free fall attempt.

It isn't quite that bad, or good, but it's awfully close. It isn't what we say, it's what we don't say. I remember one patient of mine, a middle aged lady who took an overdose of medication in a suicide attempt. We had to hospitalize her and she recovered. She also had a slight bladder infection during her hospital stay. The insurance agent reminded the husband who reminded me, "Doctor, don't put anything down about the tension she's been under or I'll have to pay the whole thing." Final diagnosis:

1. Acute urinary cystitis.
2. Adverse drug reaction.
3. Mild obesity.
4. Benign essential hypertension.

The family didn't go broke, the agent didn't lose a client, and I slept well (I think). This is all phony enough but the hospital records look like Biblical scrolls compared to office records. Again, anything related to "nerves" is not covered. So guess what. We've developed this to a fine art in the office. If 70 percent of all office visits are related to nerves, stress and anxiety as I said earlier, and I can't call them emotional, someone's got a problem, or would have a problem if doctors weren't literary greats. I could put all the patients I've diagnosed as having stress-related illness in 20 years of practice in the trunk of my Mustang. If every doctor I know collected all of the same, we would need to have two Mustangs.

The end of the horror story is that the insurance companies get all of these forms with assorted diagnosis on them, review them, and produce statistics about the health problems of this country. The net result is that there just ain't many stress-made illnesses or wheel chair syndromes running around. Clear?

But let's back up. I said doctors and attorneys are experts at easing people into the wheel chair syndromes. Doctors have numerous reasons, attorneys have only one.

Let's look at the legal interests concerning a patient, for example. Carl was 51 years old and had worked for 20 years for the same industrial plant as a truck mechanic. He developed a backache and came into see me.

"Doctor, this thing is getting me down. I've tried to work with it, but I think work is making it worse. We've got to do something or my working days are over."

I had treated Carl on occasion over the past 10 years for arthritis of the back. He did well and had no more or less than you would expect for his age. I examined him and repeated X-rays of his back and nothing had really changed.

Carl told me: "I'm reporting this as an industrial accident this time. I was using a wrench and I know that did it. I've worked for that damn company twenty years and I've never gotten a thing from them. They just gave one of the other guys an easier job that I should have had."

I could see the clouds gathering and felt his symptoms were

out of proportion to his findings. I asked an orthopedic consultant to see him and he basically agreed with my diagnosis.

Carl asked me to forward my results to the attorney that he had retained.

"My attorney said it's obvious to him that my working days are over and we're going to get a settlement and disability."

I sent my reports and knew the next chapter well. Carl came back and didn't mention the backache at all.

"My attorney wasn't too happy with your report. He says we aren't going to get anywhere with that kind of story. He says I'm never going to be able to work and you made it sound like I was nearly well."

"Well, let's see, Carl," I said. "How completely did your attorney examine you?"

"Examine me — what are you talking about? He doesn't do that!"

"That's strange," I countered. "He knows more about your medical condition than I do and he didn't even undress you."

Carl began to get the message that I was getting his and his attorney's message.

"Well anyway, no hard feelings," he said. "But my attorney wants you to send all of my X-rays and records to this doctor." He handed me a doctor's card.

I sent the records and Carl was off for three years getting "worse and worse" awaiting the disability hearing. His grown children were patients and continued to check with me. He had a small drinking problem that increased steadily as the months passed on. He gave up fishing and all of the outdoor sports that he enjoyed. He knew he was going for broke. He and the attorney had their work cut out for them. The bigger the wound, the larger the bandage. If they were going to shoot for high stakes, they had better have their homework done. They did it well and he finally got his settlement and retirement.

"Not much, but adequate," his son said. It's what doctors call the "greenback poultice." (But only in the doctor's room.) The meaning is obvious, the patient doesn't get better until the financial reward is obtained. It's one of the few known cures for certain wheel chair syndromes. Does it really work and is it foolproof or long lasting? Not in my experience. The problem is the poor patient and his legal coach go overboard. They start believing themselves. The patient wants to and the attorney has to. The attorney can afford this game, both financially and emotionally. He's going to love him and leave him after taking half the spoils. The trouble is, Carl has been playing the game for real. He's really learned how to hurt and wear his crown of thorns while the storm was brewing. He can't walk into that hearing without his misery suit on, and he doesn't. He and the attorney are in full agreement, as one of Faulkner's characters put it, "Between grief and nothing, I'll take grief." How does it end. The attorney gets something, Carl gets something plus grief. The unfortunate twist is that the "greenback poultice" only helps for a short revengeful while. The grief goes on. Why? Carl learned his part too well. He programmed his computer so well that's it's overloaded, it's spewing out all sorts of mixed-up answers to his present problem.

"How long do I keep on hurting (if I really do)? Is it okay to 'not hurt' now? If I don't hurt should I go back to work? Would I have to cut down on my drinking, would my children quit being concerned? Would I mow the lawn, and how about my fishing and carrying outboard motors. I love to fish but if I can pack a 50 pound motor down the bank — no, I don't think I'll fall for that one." And on and on. The children have been concerned, but not like Carl thinks. As his son said, "He'd be the loser if he received a million dollars." His son is right. Three years later, Carl sits in his chair in his little retirement villa and thinks all day long, pondering the sins the world has committed against him. He hasn't fished his favorite hole in 10 years, and he never will. He is in a mental wheel chair with safety belt buckled.

As one attorney friend told me, "The only one in the courtroom who wins is me, and I'm not even sure of that. I've never seen an award that was large enough to compensate for the damage the plaintiff does to himself to obtain it."

But what about doctors? We do it all the time. We are loaded with wheel chair syndrome innuendos. "Take it easy, slow down, you've got to rest more, you're doing too much, be sure and call me immediately if you're not feeling better, I don't want you going back to work for two weeks after your finger laceration." Why do we do it? I'm not sure. I think it's a role we've learned. It makes the patient dependent on us; we're in control, we'll remove all pain. I think we do this early in practice to build a practice. We act concerned. We do it these days mainly as a legal defensive measure: to stay out of court.

As one professor told us, "All doctors should have hemmorhoids and a receding hairline to look mature and concerned!" We use double standards, though.

Every doctor I know who has his hernia repaired does it at 4 p.m. on Friday afternoon and his wife drives him to the beach to recuperate over the weekend. *HE* drives back Sunday afternoon and is seeing patients Monday morning. No one usually knows he's had it done. But what about the patient that *he* operates on. That's a completely different story. The hernia is repaired on Monday morning. The patient is allowed to "dangle his toes" over the bed Monday, he can try walking (Tuesday) in the room — he makes it around the hospital corridor about mid-week and if all is well he'll be sent home Friday if he promises he won't lift anything heavier than a miniature marshmallow sack for two months. It's true. We think we are being "extra careful" in protecting the patient (and ourselves) to the fullest extent. We're not though. Every study done shows that early ambulation and resumption of activities promotes healing and well-being. After all, that's why doctors treat themselves that way. Granted we can't start lifting 100 pound sacks at work after a hernia repair but we also don't need to "move into the sick room" on first floor!

I think that this whole approach accounts for all of the doctors' waiting rooms across this country being continuously filled with people who shouldn't be there. We've got that "ain't it awful syndrome" or, as Jess Lair calls it, the "pity pot" syndrome, and the doctor has a tender ear and is going to play the game. Why not, his livelihood depends on it.

I have one patient that typifies the whole thing. He spent so long building his mental wheel chair that he is literally ready (if not overdue) for the real thing.

Ralph is 53 years old and looks 93. He has built a shrine out of his symptoms and he worships at it daily. The first time I saw Ralph he gave me a 20-minute barrage of afflictions that would wipe out the average Army battalion. He had a symptom for every organ he owned. I made the cardinal mistake of greeting him with "How are you?" I now say "Good Morning" when he comes in, but it doesn't help. He began to be a medical disaster in his early 20s. Ralph had repeated back surgeries in his 20s for herniated discs. He had surgery on his shoulder joint for chronic pain and bursitis. He had a heart attack at age 34. He had a hiatal hernia repair done later. He complained of pains in "every bone in my body." He was bothered with trembling arms and hands, fatigue, insomnia, anginal pain, elevated blood pressure and cholesterol, migraine headaches and constipation. He sat on the end of the examining table clutching his large back braces and two sacks of prescription medicines he was on. He was downcast, his voice was weak and tremulous, his brow was furrowed. In short, a more dejected, "beaten" victim of personal conflict than I had ever seen.

He slipped over his heart attack at age 34 as though it was nature's plan. I couldn't help but wonder why this hadn't caused him to examine his life at that point. It hadn't and Ralph was well on his way toward a "woe is me" life ahead. His chest pain worsened and I had him examined by a cardiologist. Ralph came back and said, "Did you hear — I damn near died on the table." (He had a cardiac catheterization done and had some extra cardiac beats and irregularity.) He then said, "The cardiologist said my heart vessels looked good. Now why would he say a thing like that?" Ralph was visibly upset. He had had 15 years of chest pain and the cardiologist undermined the whole thing. I explained to him that he did have some slight coronary narrowing but it just wasn't very bad and "that's good, isn't it?"

"Well, yes, I suppose. I mean I don't want it to be worse than it is, but I do have some then, don't I?" We cut down a lot of medication that he didn't need and he did do better for a little while. He developed an inflammatory colitis that ended up with a peritonitis and surgery. He was extremely ill. His recovery was fine but he dwelt daily on how sick he had been and repeatedly said "I nearly died, didn't I?" The situation had changed. The cardiologist and I had been telling him he was well and now he knew better. The implications I got were very clear.

"You think I'm doing pretty good, but now you know better." I had the feeling Ralph's body was accommodating his mental attitude.

Ralph has a large business and has no diversions. I tried to have him take time off, pick out a hobby, and this helped a bit. He took his first vacation in years but couldn't think of a hobby that would "interest him."

I finally told Ralph that his eight hour days were over, that he could now only work three hours a day. He came back looking like a different person. I had accidentally done the magical thing. I had placed him in the mental wheel chair. Ralph couldn't do it himself because as he repeatedly told me, "My dad told me I had to work for everything I'd ever get. He really made me independent." Independent? Ralph couldn't be further from it, but if he sees himself this way it's going to require outside help to get the wheel chair syndrome on. I obliged and he did beautifully for several months. The better he looked and felt the less concerned the whole firm showed about his health. The less concern they showed him, the worse he began to feel. To feel worse he finally went back to working long days, six days a week. Things are looking up again. He feels miserable and looks horrible. They have a bed in the plant now and "they insist I lie down if I don't look good. I wish they wouldn't worry so much about me." Should we guess about Ralph's future? Is he going to spring out of the mental wheel chair? No. He's going to graduate to the real thing if he can possibly arrange it.

How can we avoid this grand and painful plot especially with so many kind professionals and friends "helping" us slip into it? Only by deciding that we have the power and talent and beauty within us to get on to greater things. The key is "within." We're not going to find it somewhere "out there," no matter how hard we fight or how fast we run. It won't be handed to us at the doctor's office, in the courtroom, or on the analyst's couch. This isn't more bad news; it's exciting news, really. It can save a lot of blind approaches. If it's all within us, great. Now we know where to look!

When do we start? As early as we can. The first symptoms our body starts telling us about should get us interested in examining ourselves. Usually they are "gentleman's" warnings like fatigue, headache, insomnia, skin rash, upset stomach, bowel changes, etc. Sometimes it's more tragic and maybe life threatening or even fatal. That makes the minor ones all the more important to us. If we can begin to change our ways, crawl out of our ruts with a minor symptom, we may prevent the disaster down the road. We have to be able to act and this takes courage. We can't be like the patient I saw with the long standing nervous rash on his arms who tells me, "Don't worry about that, doctor, it doesn't even itch anymore. I've had it for years. The dermatologist told me 'it's my ulcer.'"

One of the biggest stumbling blocks is acceptance. Most of us say, "Wait a minute — that rash or that headache or that ulcer can't be nerves. I'm not the type." What type? I suppose they mean the "nervous type." But I can't go along with that. We're all the "nervous type." We're all built with the very same set of nerves. As one doctor said, "The only patients I have that aren't nervous are in the cemetery; for the rest of us it's just a matter of degree."

Looking cool and half asleep doesn't mean anything. I know one physician who is so calm you have to poke him to see if he's breathing, and he's had repeated bouts of bleeding ulcers. I'm sure the other hang-up is that we all feel we're strong enough and smart enough to control our nerves. It's beneath us. If we end up with an ailment caused by tension then we obviously have failed. We really weren't strong enough or smart enough.

This is nonsense. At one of our famous medical institutions, patients from all over the world are treated for all sorts of disorders, including stomach problems. A study was done there to see how many of the physicians on the staff now had or had ever had ulcers. The results: 50 percent of the entire staff.

So if we're going to avoid the one-way street we've been talking about we've got to begin to look at our symptoms and illnesses in a new light. The next time you head for the doctor's office, ask yourself, "Could I be causing my illness? Could nerves be a factor?" Remember the odds and don't leave without posing the question to the doctor if he fails to bring it up. Watch his expression. Chances are he'll look relieved even if it was your idea. You've opened the door for both of you and that's the first step. If it is tension based, look again. Now ask yourself, 'What's in it for me? What am I getting from it. Do I have an illness or have I 'become an illness.' Is the illness using me or am I using the illness? Is the sickness worth the misery? Is the misery worth any possible rewards?"

3 – Those Unsympathetic Nerves

*Doctors pronounce many diseases incurable, and often
in the rest err and fail to cure.*

Frances Bacon

By now I'm sure that most readers are wondering if I even
believe in the "germ theory." Don't bacteria really exist, and
aren't they at least partly to blame for the world's maladies?
Bacteria are alive and well and have their troops marshalled against
us, it's true, and I believe in the whole concept. Pasteur knew
whereof he spoke. I'm just putting it in a different light. I'm
convinced that it's a one-sided battle. The bacteria don't have to
"attack us." We get ourselves so emotionally and physically
defeated that we literally invite them in. Think how you felt
before you got your last cold, or pneumonia or bladder infection.
Had you changed jobs, or sold your house, or headed a church
bazaar, or were you getting married or divorced?

Most studies that have been carefully done invariably show
that a stressful time or event usually precedes an illness. We'll look
at one excellent study of this later.

For now, let's use Jerry for an example. Jerry is 16 years old
and I have taken care of him since he was an infant. He has been
healthy and has never had any respiratory problems. All of a
sudden I had him in the hospital three times for pneumonia in a
nine month period. The logical medical question is, "Why?" Or, as
the parents firmly put it to me, "Doctor, what else should you be
looking for or doing for Jerry?"

The question is well put, but I take it a bit on the defense.
We had done all the usual tests and examinations to see if
something was contributing to these recurrent infections. Everything was normal. I asked the parents if there were problems at
home or at school and was told "Heavens no, Jerry is a good
student and you know our family." I did know the family and
that's what bothered me. Jerry's hair was gradually lengthening
over the past two years and father's crew cut was getting
progressively shorter. Dad's visits to the hospital bothered me.
Jerry basked in them. Dad had to sit two feet away and look at
Jerry and his long hair, and still be nice. After all, Jerry's darned
sick. I could feel sparks in the air and again talked with mother
and dad on Jerry's third hospital admission.

"Everything's fine. Couldn't be better. You just get Jerry
well this time for good." Three months later the parents appeared
in my office asking for help.

"Doctor, we've got a problem. We found marijuana in Jerry's

room a year ago. He knows that we know but we haven't said anything. We need your help." Jerry and the parents have had a stressful past year and Jerry's body wasn't taking it.

How does this all work? How does Jerry's marijuana and Dad's crew cut add up to pneumonia for Jerry? It seems like a strange and improbable equation. The small responsible bacterium, the pneumococcus that caused Jerry's pneumonia, knows precious little about the use of marijuana or hair styles in this world. Besides, these bugs or bacteria have probably been around since time began and they can't bank their entire survival on a passing hair style or someone's interest in a mind bending drug.

Bacteria may not be the smartest observers of the passing social scene but don't underestimate them. They do know when the social scene has someone against the ropes and it's time for the knockout punch.

Belittle the bacteria all you like but don't underestimate the timing mechanism of these little microscopic characters.

If you and I were as small as these lowly bacteria with only one cell and could only be seen under a microscope, we'd travel in pairs and know something about our 150 lb. opponents.

Bacteria, like any predator or killer, know exactly when to strike. I see these bacteria circling their victim much like the coyotes do an isolated cow or calf in a Charles Russell painting. The coyotes don't usually take on the entire herd and neither do the bacteria. They both select a special victim to move in on, one that somehow looks a little weaker or seems less able to defend itself.

In medical terms we talk about "host resistance" or immunity. We're talking about the ability of the host (more appropriately the victim) to defend itself. Lowering of the host resistance is the necessary ingredient we must add to complete our equation. "Victim plus pneumococcal bacteria equals pneumonia." Jerry's host resistance or immunity has got to somehow be lowered before the pack moves in and Jerry has obliged. He has literally been cut from the herd, or separated from the family. The year-long conflict has lowered his host resistance. His immunity is down so much that the bacteria take him on three times in a nine-month period and win.

Jerry has an unresolved conflict. He's smoking marijuana and he's pretty sure his parents know. He's darned sure they don't approve but no one is talking. And this goes on an entire year. Plenty of flyers have been sent out but no one is reading them because no one can handle the message. It's what I call the grey zone or the ulcer zone of conflict. We could call it the decision zone or the indecision zone just as well.

Whatever we call it, it's a destructive resistance lowering force at work. To me it's better to make a "wrong" decision than to wait too long to make any decision at all.

Jerry and his parents have got to make some decisions. Does Jerry hang up his marijuana habit or do the parents state their case? Do they move Jerry out or accept his habit? And what about mom and dad? Aren't they weakened too with all this? The bacteria must sense that they have three victims isolated in the same household. Shouldn't they have a picnic or at least a small epidemic? Maybe they realize that at least mother and dad have each other to talk to. Two victims may be a small herd, but it's apparently safer than standing alone with only your conflict.

Whatever the bacteria had in mind, mom and dad didn't get pneumonia. Dad had to settle for a moderate elevation of his cholesterol level and mother developed hypertension.

We've been so slow to accept this approach to disease because it's hard to measure. We can't bottle it or x-ray it. We can't vaccinate against it.

We know a sneeze droplet can travel up to twelve miles. We've tagged a sneeze droplet with a radioactive tracer and measured its course.

How does anyone escape? Before Jenner introduced smallpox vaccination, every sailing ship would lose half of its crew once smallpox broke out on board ship. Here we have twenty or thirty men caged up in a small sailing vessel and yet only half of them die with smallpox. If the virus is so infectious and epidemic in nature, why doesn't the entire crew succumb?

It's the same in the prisoner of war camps, as Victor E. Frankhl so graphically describes in his book *Man's Search for Meaning*. Most of the prisoners were treated with the same deprivations. Yet many of the prisoners died of starvation and disease while other prisoners spent their time nursing their dying comrades and survived the ordeal.

In medical jargon we would say the survivors must have a natural immunity or resistance. But if it's so natural, why doesn't everyone have it?

Maybe this is what Virey, the 17th century physician, alluded to when he said, "Civilized man has lost this instinct of health and it is now the business of science to rediscover for him in the form of exact knowledge the biological wisdom that once was his birthright."

Maybe this is why, despite all of our medical conquests of these infectious diseases, we can't build hospitals fast enough to accommodate the sick and why the national health care costs are sickening to everyone.

Let's take a look at our nervous system. I'm not going to drag you through a long clinical thriller of medical jargon, but we do have to lay down a bit of basic groundwork so that the following chapters will make sense and seem plausible when we connect your decreasing marital bliss to your increasing number of health problems. So hang with me for a short story about our nervous system.

You and I have nerve fibers running to every organ, every extremity and every square inch of our skin. We have motor nerves that leave our brain and run down our spinal cord to our face, arms, legs, our chest and back and abdomen. We can control all these nerves at will if they are normal and haven't been injured by disease or accident. If we want to frown or smile we do it, if we want to bend our back or raise an arm or leg we do it. We don't even have to plan it too much in detail, but we do have to make the decision or nothing happens. The decision can be made extremely rapidly, as when we duck our head to save a black eye. Sometimes we're a bit late but we usually move pretty fast without much hesitation.

We've developed these motor nerves to some amazing degrees. We can catch a baseball on the run, play the violin, catch a trapeze bar in mid air, etc. To watch a talented pianist play the piano and see the fingers fly would make us think the fingers rolled automatically. They do — almost. Yet if we transplanted these "talented hands" to another person's wrists whose nervous system was not finely trained we would have a sad performance. As effortless and as automatic as it seems, it isn't; each note and each motion is a decision. These, then, are the nerves regulating muscle activity that we control all day long. They respond only to our conscious decisions.

The other portions of our nervous system have long names, the sympathetic and the parasympathetic nervous system. This portion of the nervous system is also referred to as the autonomic, or self-governing nervous system. Don't worry about these long names. These are nerves that also leave the brain and run via the spinal cord to every portion of our body. They are more concerned with controlling the heart, lungs, stomach, kidneys, intestines, urinary bladder and blood vessels. These are the silent guardians that tell the heart to continue beating at a rate *THEY* decide on, that tell the lungs to take another breath (hopefully), that tell the urinary bladder it is time to be emptied, and likewise the colon. They also tell the arteries and the skin to open up and dissipate some body heat, if it is hot out, or to constrict and save body heat if it's a cold day. These nerves are not always accommodating. They may make us cough during the "silent moment of prayer" or may paralyze our vocal cords when we get so "mad I couldn't talk."

They make us sneeze if the wrong pollen comes along and our nose becomes a faucet. They cause our skin to stand up in terror, or "goosepimples," when our mother-in-law steps off the plane. They cause our face to turn red with a compliment or an insult or white with fear, again as I mentioned previously, by causing the muscles in the arteries to open or constrict. They turn on tears at the most unscheduled times and sometimes seem confused. We usually find tears welling up with sadness but very often they're tears of joy. They're not consistent with us. (After twenty years of marriage to a certain blond I'm convinced that some people have more control over their "tear mechanism" than was previously thought possible.)

These nerves control our saliva and gastric secretions. They can dry our mouth and throat when we're nervous. Have you noticed the inevitable glass of water on the speaker's stand? Are speakers nervous or are they just always dehydrated? These nerves can make our underarms and palms moist at the most inopportune times even while making the mouth dry. They can cause all of our blood vessels to dilate at once and throw us into shock which is what happens when we faint. They cause us to yawn and to shiver.

These, then, are the sympathetic and the parasympathetic nerves at work. They are well formed at birth and begin to do their jobs those first two years with amazing ease. Some of them need a little coaxing and we call that "potty training." The bladder and lower colon do their job, they just aren't too selective as to when they do it those first few months. This is also when we start goofing things up if we are not careful. If the "potty training" becomes a premier performance each day and Johnnie is to perform his daily duty when mother plays a certain record on the stereo (don't laugh, it happens) then Johnnie may be carrying a small portable tape recorder to the biffy with him each day in college. This may sound absurd but it isn't. I have one mother, age 80, who faithfully brings in Bobby, her son, age 60, to discuss his bowel irregularity.

If we don't allow our sympathetic and parasympathetic nervous systems to work in peace, they can rapidly become the "unsympathetic" nervous systems, and this is what happens all too often. They have also been called the "uncontrollable" nerves, but we're beginning to see that that isn't quite right. We can send them so many wrong suggestions that they absolutely rebel and turn against us. Maybe we'd be better off without this part of the nervous system if they're going to work against us.

Yet we need these nerves to keep urging another heartbeat, another breath, another appetite and we need a little advance warning if our bladder or colon are full. If only we could eliminate the ones that make us blush, or sneeze or burp, or cause our stomach to overproduce acid, etc. But we can't make a deal with our nervous system, we're stuck with it, "sympathetic" or "unsympathetic."

We do have a few outs. We can have the surgeons help us a bit. They can cut the nerves that run to the remaining section of stomach when they remove a portion for the ulcer. That cuts down the acid flow and we may prevent another ulcer. The trouble is that just lets us concentrate on fouling up some other portion of the remaining nerves in the "unsympathetic" nervous system. It's like buying pails to place around the house to fix a leaky roof.

One 52-year-old lady demonstrates this so well. She had had headaches for seven years, along with "a tight neck." She had tried the usual assortment of medications and therapies that I could think of, as well as those of the neurologist and orthopedic consultants. The consultants and I felt it was tension at work, but Gloria wouldn't consider this possibility, saying "I even have these headaches on vacation." Finally she found a neurosurgeon, on her own, who cast new light in Gloria's world. He felt she needed a surgical procedure on her neck to fuse two vertebrae, not a re-organization of her life style. The surgery was accomplished, and two months later, Gloria came in, without the headache.

She was relieved, but not without doubt. "Do you know Doctor X?" she asked. "He must be good, because all the patients on my floor of the hospital were his patients. I had a funny feeling about the whole thing, somehow, but whether he's scalpel happy or not, he has sure helped me. I'm so relieved. But, are you ready for this? I've had diarrhea and stomach cramps for the past month. It's been so bad I've been afraid to leave the bathroom. I've never had anything like this in my life. What's the matter with me, anyway?"

All I could think of was a warning I heard from a professor while I was in medical school: "Never remove a patient's symptoms that are caused by emotions or stress without getting to the cause, or the patient will develop something worse in place of the original ailment." It seemed confusing at the time, but it's so obvious now. When the automatic nervous system has "had it," the only way it has for registering that something is wrong is by giving us symptoms. Trying to cover the symptoms, the attention-getting device of our automatic nerves, is like placing the classroom agitator in a dunce cap and sitting him in the corner so he doesn't disrupt the class. He'll get more attention and disrupt things more in the corner than he ever did at his desk.

Let's review for a minute. We've decided that all of us can control one portion of our nervous system and all of us can't control the rest. Now that covers everyone doesn't it? We haven't left out anyone. So the next time one of us decide that we aren't the "nervous type" we're setting ourselves up as a medical oddity. As I said before, we're all the nervous type. We can't be "non-nervous." We don't have to shake from head to toe to be the nervous type that we all have mental pictures of. I know I am arguing the point but it is important. I'll grant you that some of us have converted our sympathetic nerves to be a little less sympathetic, but we all have the same potential. We're all in this together and with the right set of circumstances our nervous system can be just as unsympathetic as it desires and so often this is just what happens.

As Sir William Osler said: "The load of tomorrow, added to that of yesterday, carried today makes the strongest falter."

So, from here on, let's forget "types." They don't apply and I don't like them. Neurotics, obsessives, hypochondriacs, we've got an endless list of names for people who are losing in our social war. In medical school we used the term "crock." This applied to any patient whose symptoms we couldn't understand or couldn't relieve.

Why do physicians reject patients whose problems seem resistant to care? Because the doctor has his pride. What would an architect do if his buildings kept falling over? Console himself with "try, try again?" No. He'd curse the "stupid workers" and leave town.

I'm suggesting that these uncontrollable nerves might not be so uncontrollable after all. That's what it's all about. If we had no control at all, we couldn't convert them into "unsympathetic" nerves and we could stop right here. I've had numerous patients approach me with, "I know you're right. I know what the problems are. I know what's upsetting me. I know what's making me this way, but where is the 'key' to all this?" The patients have a good point. It's easy to say that our actions are burning a hole in our stomach or duodenum, an ulcer in the making, or that our reactions to our day is causing it, but how do we get out of this pattern? Where is the "key"? None of us do it on purpose. I'm totally convinced that no one in this world gets up each morning to see how lousy a day we can have, or create. It just wouldn't make sense. Yet that's exactly what we so often do.

As C. J. Jung the noted psychologist said, "It is not I who created myself; rather, I happened to myself."

I tell my patients and myself that we shouldn't be so interested in finding a key. We should decide to understand the tumbler mechanism of the lock. In other words, if we know how the lock works, what the inner mechanism is like, maybe we can pick away at it even if we don't find the "key." I'm not sure a "key" exists. It's the tumblers that count and we each have to work out our own combination for our individual lock. I think the comparison fits because we really do have ourselves locked in and are usually afraid to even consider a new combination approach to the way we are seeing things. We must.

Many of my patients have trouble writing their "life story" for me. This is a device that has been a real help to both me and the patient. What I really want is an autobiographical sketch of the important events in a patient's life. What's important? Anything that comes to mind. And, it never fails to be important to both of us. I like to know about the patient's dreams, conquests, defeats, and relationships with friends and family, and I've found that if the patient does it in the quiet of home, without having to "make conversation" with me it is a saving of time for me and money for the patient. But, the reaction frequently is the same:

"I don't think I can do that."

"Do what? Write about me?"

"What will I say?"

"What if I write the wrong things?"

I purposely leave the directions vague except to tell them that most people write between ten and twenty pages. This is a start for them and only fifty percent will do it. The rest say that they tried or that they wrote the life story and threw it away because I wouldn't have liked it. Who wouldn't have liked what? How could they write the wrong story and who decides? I think they approach writing about life just as they approach living it: Doubtful, insecure, unsure what someone will say, needing approval. Several patients have asked if I would still continue to take care of them after seeing their "life story." Frequently they write things down that they haven't openly thought about or talked about for years. The patients often tell me the same thing: "My life story was so painful to write, but I felt good after I finished it. I couldn't believe some of the things that came to mind!"

There is an old cliche about blood being thicker than water. I used to think I knew what it meant, that a blood bond was a helpful, cohesive bond between people that few things could come between. Now, I'm not so sure. Blood can thicken to the point where it doesn't flow at all, and two or more persons suffer because of it. So often I see this blood relationship being more of a divider than a constructive bond between members of a family. The feelings they write about have been down there smouldering away, creating anxiety and unhappiness, giving the unsympathetic nervous system a real whee of a time. It's the buried emotions that hurt. Once we get them dusted off we can begin to take control!

Often I don't need a "life story"; a short story will do. One 19-year-old boy came to me with painful headaches at the base of his skull. On examination I found that he had severe hypertension. His blood pressure was 240/110 which is very high and dangerous. He is a candidate for a stroke even at his young age. I did the usual workup and there was no renal or adrenal gland cause for it. He had what is called "benign essential hypertension." This is the type millions of people have. I think the label is a bit odd. Benign means harmless and essential means necessary.

I told him that the tests were all normal and he accepted it.

"It's me, doctor," he assured me. "My mother and I don't get along. She's so domineering and she has been all my life. I can't wait to get out on my own."

I put him on blood pressure pills and it came down somewhat. I added more medication and we finally got it down to 160/90 which was still too high. He followed closely for a while and we barely kept it under control. It never got below 160/90. He finally quit coming in. One year later he returned and told me that he had been married and had had a complete "falling out" with his mother. He told his mother that he would not see her again unless she let him and his new wife lead their own lives. He hadn't seen her for months. To my surprise his blood pressure was 130/80, perfectly normal. I was more surprised when he told me that he had stopped his blood pressure pills shortly after he moved away from home and hadn't taken one since.

"I knew I didn't need them anymore. I could feel it change the day I left home," he said. "I knew I was well so I just stopped the pills but I thought I should check with you just to make sure," he said.

He was right. He was well. He had found a new combination for the lock. Don't misunderstand. I'm not recommending marriage to cure anything (please read Chapter 6 before even considering it), but getting married and leaving his parents' home cured his "benign essential hypertension." It wasn't benign, he didn't need it and four years later he doesn't have it.

This demonstrates so well the control we really do have over these "uncontrollable" nerves. We can't tell the nerves to relax the small muscles in our arteries and lower the blood pressure but we can change some things in our life patterns and "allow it to occur." This is a crucial point. The body is really quite remarkable. It wants to run smoothly. It tries to make the right corrections. It knows when it's not working in our best interest and it even tells us so. As Jung also said, "There is no illness that is not at the same time an unsuccessul attempt at a cure."

If our blood pressure is markedly elevated, we get a headache. If our stomach is turning out too much acid, it hurts, if our nervous system is frayed we feel weak and exhausted. Remember how good you and I felt as small children before we started goofing things up?

Our bodies are continually sending messages to our "control panel." All we have to do is check the panel now and then. Watch for the red light, our symptoms. If they're flashing a stomach ache, skin rash, dizziness, headache or whatever, we've got to start checking trouble areas in our day. We can't do this by taking pills to "numb" the control panel. It's like disconnecting the "stall buzzer" on an airplane so it will stop annoying us. It's just as dangerous.

I have seen enough people begin to control these unsympathetic nerves that I know it's possible. It's hard and that's why we have 2.8 million people marching into doctor's offices each day. I'm also convinced that the longer we wait to take control the harder it becomes and I see many patients that will never change.

I like to compare "taking control" of our bodies with throwing a "master mental switch" on the control panel. I even tell people to consider an electrical panel box with a large handle on it. When things get too dark, when doubt piles up too high, when symptoms start mounting up, throw the switch to the other position. I know it sounds fuzzy, but it works. Try it. Halfway through a lousy day (or sooner) stop and tell yourself "I'm going to make this a beautiful day, come what may." It works. I've done it many times and I hope to have to do it less and less. I know you're wondering, how can I turn a day around when things are piling up at work, or the dog bit the neighbor boy or I got rear-ended at the intersections. Let me tell you how one patient does it.

Neil is a very wealthy man in his mid-fifties. He found religion a little late and consequently grabbed a larger portion. More power to him. The point is he was able to put it to work for him. His past is a mess and he's trying to correct it. His business was getting him down and he works extremely long hours. His health was failing rapidly and his family was coming apart in the process.

One day he came in looking great and told me he had developed an entirely new philosophy.

"When I get up in the morning," he said, "I know the good Lord has my work cut out for me. I know I will encounter problems all day long and it is my job to meet and solve them. Then during the day when such a problem comes along I say, see, another one just as planned and I proceed to solve it with all the ability I have. On the days that I don't have problems I'm pleased. I call these my 'bonus days.' You'd be amazed, doctor, at how many 'bonus days' I'm beginning to have."

He threw the switch. Just a mental jolt, a different way of reacting to the control panel. I'm sure his bonus days will continue to increase. The problems are the same, he just reacts differently to them. His health improved dramatically over the last few years. He didn't find the key to a trouble-free world; he just tried using a different approach to his day.

A lady came to me requesting a prescription of "Empirin No. 3" (empirin and codeine). She was 47 and stated that she had had severe headaches and had taken four to six empirin No. 3s as long as she could remember. I explained to her that I would not prescribe them for her and that she was taking too many. She was upset but we had a long talk. She poured out a tearful story about her teenage years with an amorous stepfather which she had never told "anyone." Just relating the story relaxed her visibly, and she left after agreeing to try getting by without the codeine. She came in some time later just to thank me. She looked remarkably better. We read her chart together on the first and only time that I had seen her. It was full of comments that I had made, "weepy, shaking, apprehensive lady with long-standing headaches, complains of 'hot flashes,' fainting spells and weakness, addicted to codeine."

She broke out laughing, "That was me, wasn't it?"

She said, "Just getting something like that out of you is half the battle, isn't it?"

It was the whole battle for her. I've seen her since for examinations and she hasn't taken an Empirin No. 3 since. She had to bring things to the surface.

I don't mean to make this all sound easy and simple to do. It isn't. It is easy to at least check the control panel and see if any of the lights are on. It may help if we know which lights are most likely to flash.

The most common symptom, or panel light, I see is fatigue in both men and women. So watch for it — do you have it now? I don't mean the kind of fatigue you get after digging all day in the garden, that's natural. I'm talking about the fatigue patients describe when they say, "Doctor, I'm tired when I get up, I'm dragging all day, I fall into bed at night, I think I'm more tired in the morning than when I went to bed." I've had it and so have you. This is pure emotional drain. Your body is burning carbohydrate at an alarming rate and it can't keep up with you. It's worse than climbing mountains.

I have, at times, looked at the carpet on my office floor and thought, if only the waiting room would evaporate and I could lie down for a two-day nap. The trouble is, it would only help while I was asleep. Once I wake up I'm right back facing problems improperly. You and I are causing it, it's emotional and not excess physical labor. It always amazes me how exhausting it is to make an early morning medical call five miles away and how refreshing it is to leave just as early and drive 100 miles to go fishing.

What's the next light to start blinking? The stomach and colon are the next most common set of symptoms I see. Watch the television ads competing for "stomach ache" dollars and you'll agree. Drug companies would not be spending millions of dollars on advertisements for indigestion aids if they weren't getting their money back tenfold. Indigestion, gas, stomach or lower colon cramps, bloating, and diarrhea or constipation. We spend over 125 million dollars on laxatives alone in this country each year. These are miserable symptoms and we've all had some of them I'm sure.

These are the symptoms that lead to the upper and lower "GI" X-ray studies and the sigmoidoscopic examinations. These exams show a variety of things. The most common finding is "nothing." We don't call it that because normal reports are no fun and we don't want to hear it. Neither do insurance companies want to pay for "nothing" on the insurance form. If we're going to subject ourselves to all these indiscretions, we better get something to show for it.

As one lady said after I'd told her that the stomach X-rays were normal. "They're what? *Normal?* Nothing is wrong? Well, okay, but please don't tell my husband."

So we find something most of the time. Such things as "probable gastritis (inflammed stomach wall), irritable duodenum, possible small hiatal hernia, slow emptying stomach, spastic colon or tortuous colon (whose isn't)." Sometimes we do better if the unsympathetic nerves have really been working overtime. Then we may well find an ulcer. If we do find an ulcer, everyone's excited about it and we dash down the hall and show the X-rays to the patient and point with satisfaction right to the ulcer "shadow." We don't usually show the tortuous colon films; we just put it on the insurance forms so no one accuses us of treating something mental or emotional.

I saw one radiologist practically doing handstands in anger one morning at the hospital.

"Why does the staff keep ordering all these unnecessary damned upper and lower 'GIs'." That stopped me for a minute. How can he complain? That's his living, the more the merrier. The doctor had good reason. He knew most of them were normal and he was tired of looking through Roget's Thesaurus to find a new way to say something about nothing. If *he* can't take it, how about the patient, who gets the "raw thrill" *plus* the bill?

I'm not saying that the gastritis and colitis aren't real. Far from it. They are real problems and cause much suffering. What is important is that we place things in perspective. We shouldn't have to see "something" on the X-ray to make us change our style. The pain alone should do it. And we can't assume that we're a little strange if we hurt and the X-rays are normal. It's just that we're way ahead of the game, we're going to change our ways before our stomach or colon become extensively damaged.

We can't start treating *only* the symptoms; we've got to treat the cause.

It's not just a matter of diet. The general rule is to stop eating whatever you have been, it probably caused it, especially spices and roughage. This was in vogue for many years. Now we're turning it all around. The new thing in gastroenterology is to eat anything that isn't nailed down, the more roughage the better, and besides it just might prevent cancer of the colon. (A current passing theory.)

One recent medical journal was devoted to diseases of the colon. The first half of the journal had several articles promoting the concept of "more roughage for all" to decrease the incidence of colitis and to cause less bowel irritations in general. The last part of the journal consisted of articles about diagnosing colon troubles. The authors there told how important they felt it was to place the patient on plenty of roughage a few days before a barium enema or a sigmoidoscopic exam of the colon, "to help identify any inflamed areas or to activate bleeding in the colon so that the specific site could be more easily identified." In other words, the roughage would worsen the condition and make it easier to diagnose. Confusing? You bet, and maybe that accounts for the 34 different "life-saving" diet books I counted on one paperback stand at a local book store not long ago.

I doubt that the new dietary fads will be any more successful than those in the past. I am more inclined to believe as someone said, "It's not what you eat, it's what's eating you."

It seems confusing, doesn't it? But let's get back to basics. It's the "uncontrollables" again, the unsympathetics in action. It's our "gut reaction." You've heard it lots, I'm sure. We even project this onto other people that we're mad at. We don't hate them; we hate "their guts." The net result is even worse. It ends up with "our guts" hating "their guts." What worse affliction could we possibly cast on them? The problem is "our guts" take the rap and that's rough.

The gut reaction can be very serious and result in a fatal colitis. One patient of mine was a vivacious 56-year-old lady who was the neighborhood bright spot and had a total charm about her. She developed abdominal cramps after her husband suffered a stroke. She worried incessantly about his condition and developed a severe colitis. Her colon started pouring out protein and blood that she could not afford to lose.

She perforated through the bowel wall and we were forced to operate before we could attempt to build her up. She died two days later, three months from the day her husband had his stroke. His stroke caused her stress, which caused her death in three short months. Numerous friends of hers came to ask me how it could possibly happen. She was the "picture of health."

The third most common warning light I see is a skin rash. We call it a "neuro-dermatitis" which simply means a tension-caused rash. It's the most common rash I see by far. It itches and nothing seems to stop it. It's usually in one area at first, a localized red area, but it can rapidly spread over the entire body if the situation warrants it. This rash is all too often labeled "allergy" and a decade of shots begin. Dermatologists treat allergies and eczema, not stress.

Evelyn's case demonstrates this beautifully. Evelyn is a 41-year-old lady who had "lived" at the medical school clinics for two years fighting a generalized skin rash. She had been thoroughly examined in several of the clinics and had gone through extensive allergy testing. It was decided that she had a "metal allergy to copper and nickel." Lately the rash had localized to her hands. She came in wearing gloves because she wasn't to touch metal doorknobs of any sort. On examination her hands demonstrated a chronic case of screaming nerves — or neurodermatitis.

She was on pills and creme and allergy shots which she was refusing to go along with after two years of treatment. We started talking. Her husband was a pillar in the church but had driven all the children to live at friends' houses because of his halo. I had treated him for ulcers (unsuccessfully) a short time before. Evelyn had worked for ten years and had turned every paycheck promptly over to him. He insisted that she do so. She hadn't been allowed to buy a new dress in two years. He even accused her of enjoying her work. She was literally at the end of her unsympathetic wits.

I asked her if she had talked to him about any of this.
She answered, "NO."
Why? "I'm afraid to," she said.
"Afraid of what?" I asked. "What have you got to lose?"
She started laughing out loud until tears came. "I guess I didn't want to make it worse," she said, with her eyes still wet.

I told her it couldn't get worse, they had essentially lost their children, their love, their fun, their respect, now what do you have to lose? The ship has sunk, it's time to start rescue attempts!

The next time she came in she had on a pretty new outfit, a smile to match and rapidly healing "glove free" hands. She got a job at the bank handling nickels by the sackful and her hands healed completely. They started to work on problems at home. No one had asked her about any of this during two years of care. She didn't offer it "because it didn't seem important to anyone."

I've shown you the three most common symptoms or panel lights that I see: fatique, stomach and bowel disorders and skin rash. These three bring most patients in. We could go on and on. Headaches, I'm sure, are the most common symptom resulting from tension but these are usually treated at home unless they become progressively severe. The ones we've discussed are all caused by those supposedly "uncontrollable" nerves. It's your panel to watch and your symptoms to relieve. No one can do it for you. You can get temporary relief with medication but remember we're treating the end results not the cause when we treat symptoms. We're disconnecting the panel.

Don't drive your doctor to "find something." He's looking

furiously enough in that direction. That is the way we're trained. If he doesn't, the next doctor will. If you keep looking for a label that you can live with you'll find it I'm sure and it won't take long. As Benjamin Franklin said, "Nothing is more fatal to your health than the over care of it."

You've got to ask why that control panel is blinking all the time and then be prepared to make some changes. If I've got a symptom, I probably caused it. It's hard to take the step and cross the line, but it's beautiful on the other side.

Doctors are going to have to "tune in" with you. We've proved the old system isn't working. We are going to have to start treating patients not "cases," and causes, not symptoms.

I recently saw an article in a medical magazine entitled, "Physicians' Image May Be Slipping." The article presented a study done by Dr. Kent L. Granzin, Ph.D., and Erhard K. Valentin. Many persons were interviewed in an attempt to determine what complaints they had about physicians. What did their research reveal? What do patients find lacking in their doctor?

"Patients want their doctor to be more available, easy to talk to, interested, kind, and sympathetic than he actually appears. Patients feel they deserve considered attention for their money and will be dissatisfied until they receive it. The patients also felt the doctor should show a sense of humor since patients seem to be aware that though medicine is a serious business, they often need 'psychic relief' in the form of smiles, cheerful remarks and brighter, friendly surroundings. They also felt that physicians could show somewhat more interest in religion, at least from the point of view of some patients."

We've got to get those unsympathetic nerves back on our side. We're going to have to quit dividing up the body and deciding it's "mental" or "organic." It's not really possible to do this anyway. Every physician has to know that each of us has both body and mind and they cannot be separated in the least degree. The problem is we've set up our whole medical system on the basis that we can. Look at all our specialties and more new ones are forming all the time to further stake out claims to a certain limited area of the body. Medical students get this early in training. Is it "mental" or "physical" and worse yet, if it's "physical" that's great, we can test and treat and play scientist. If it looks "mental" (meaning we can't get a positive test or a lesion on X-ray) we'll send the patient to the "psyche" department. Isn't that what it's for?

I was working with junior and senior medical students and trying to get this point across. I presented the hypothetical case of a man with an ulcer. I told them that he has pains and an ulcer on X-ray. I asked what we should do next. The answers were logical and to the point. Bland diet, anti-acids and a medication to slow up the acid formation in the stomach. I said fine, he gets better and four months later he comes back in, it's acting up again. What now? Again they all agreed, another upper "GI," strict diet, more anti-acids and medications to slow down the acid formation in the stomach. I continued this story having the patient "in trouble" every four months. The response from the students was the same each time and I kept pressing. After every blood test and gastro scopic test known to medical science was proposed and two and one-half years later in the story, I finally gave up.

I asked, "Isn't there anything else anyone can think of to do for this poor fellow?"

Finally, one brave student asked, "Well, what are you getting at? Do you mean we ought to ask if something is 'bugging' him?"

Plato said, "The cause of many diseases is unknown to the physicians because they are ignorant of the whole."

We will continue to be ignorant of the whole person until we at least begin to ask, "How is it with you?" or "How are things going?" It's astonishing how much the patient will offer if just given the chance. One new patient caught me a bit off guard when I walked into the examining room. "Doctor," he said, "can we please *just talk*? No tests or anything? I've had twenty-two upper GI's in the past five years, and I still have a stomach ache." No one had asked him what was "bugging him," but he decided it was time to tell someone without being asked.

Doctors and medical students are really not so ignorant of the whole person anymore. We just act like it. We're so much more comfortable with our search for organic diseases. It's easier to prescribe a pill than to help someone change a life style, and unfortunately, that solution also is more acceptable to most patients.

The final obstruction is the insurance form game. Remember, we can't mention stress or emotional illness to the insurance company, or lots of bills are going to be unpaid. If the stress leads to an ulcer, that's fine. Now we have an organic disease — a hole in the stomach, and the insurance company will pay gladly. But, try billing the insurance company for an "anxiety state" or a depression leading to the ulcer!

The insurance companies have got to get "in tune." I know they return one-third of our insurance dollars to us and that's wonderful. They also are controlling our health patterns in a way I don't care for. It's turned the whole thing into a turkey raffle or a lottery. If you get the right number (organic disease) you win. If you get the wrong number (tension illness) you lose. It's like a casino. They define the game, decide the value of the chips, and decide when the game starts and stops. The game stops if the patient begins to show up too often at the "pay out" window with a "winning" diagnosis. The fact that he or she has paid premiums for thirty years before the first "win ticket" has nothing to do with it. So as I said, doctors and their secretaries have learned how to play the game since three out of four illnesses are related to stress in origin. I personally don't want a special area in Hell reserved for doctors and their secretaries. Neither the medical profession nor the insurance companies are facing reality. If three out of four patients need a policy that covers tension-caused illnesses, that's what they ought to have, or nothing. How can we even approach a problem if we can't accept the fact that it exists? It's all quite obvious. We literally can't afford to have a stress-caused illness.

This has caused the government considerable concern and we now have medicare because so many patients were "not covered" when they needed it most. How has it worked? As expected. We now have private insurance with the government helping to pay the piper, and select the "tunes." It's a bit like asking your cat to take care of your pet mouse while you're away on vacation. National health is going to be the next solution. How will that work? It's like getting a bigger cat for more protection!

If we continue to pretend that our sympathetic and "unsympathetic" nervous systems are not doing us "in" it becomes irrelevant as to who picks up the tab. No one is going to be able to keep picking up the tab anyway, whether private or government insurance.

What would be wrong with trying to eliminate 75 percent of the tab by allowing people to get well by pointing out and treating the cause, not chasing the symptoms? A radiologist friend of mine tells me 75 percent of all the X-rays he does are normal. The head of a large private laboratory says 90 percent of the tests they do are completely normal. Maybe that's why one study done at one of our major teaching medical institutions revealed that a large number of laboratory tests that were ordered by the doctors in training were never even looked at. How often would you check the hen house if 9 days out of 10 there were no eggs.

Dr. Kerr L. White, Professor of Medical Care at Johns Hopkins Medical School, says the same thing in reverse, "I don't think that more than 20 percent of what is done by doctors, nurses, etc., does any more good than harm, or use than uselessness." The percentages all add up really. If we only do more good than harm 20 percent of the time, we're leaving 80 percent of the patients out in the cold. That's the 70 to 80 percent that I'm talking about. These are the ones that we're treating for the wrong ailments with the wrong tools.

This may explain a study that revealed that the Australian aborigine witch doctor has about a 70 percent cure rate of all his patients. If our percentages have been right so far, he can't lose, can he. He must be treating the right illnesses with the right tools.

I think he could probably beat our percentage of cure rate. If you and I have an illness that is a result of stress or anxiety, boredom or depression, and will cure itself if we only "allow it," wouldn't a half hour spent with a gaily-bedecked healer, who was loaded with herbs and dancing talent, be therapeutic?

I'm not belittling the aborigine witch doctor. I can't afford to, as I'll never catch up with his impressive cure rate. But I do think we could approach at least a 69 percent cure rate if we would only take the same one half hour once in a while to start examining and treating ourselves.

So the spotlight then swings back to you and me. Are we going to use more and more drugs to short-circuit the warning lights on the control panel?

Dr. Richard Gubner, a professor of pharmacology at New York Medical College, said, "Today we can control high blood pressure with a *therapeutic barrage* which is changing the outlook for hypertensive patients from such disasters as stroke or heart attack into the prospect of a symptom free, therapeutically controlled, virtually normal state of good health."

If that's "normal good health," bring on the witch doctor. I'll take the herbs and funny mask over the "therapeutic barrage."

The Federal Drug Administration is deeply concerned about the "therapeutic barrage" that we are all subjected to. The administration is distressed about the great number of drugs in the "therapeutically controlled" of our world. The Drug Administration's concern is proper, but it is misplaced. The main concern should be with *"how come"* not *"how much."*

Every drug that is approved for public use must be found to be "safe and efficacious." Alcohol is under strict government control and has been approved for human consumption in quantities limited only by the size of one's purse. It is, then, obviously safe and its effectiveness has been proven. It "does its job" and there are "few harmful side effects reported." A prescription is not needed and you may refill it as often as you like for "therapeutic control."

One of my patients works in the pharmacy of a large supermarket chain. She told me the company has one employee who does nothing but inventory tranquilizers on hand one day a week. I couldn't help reminding her that in my neighborhood we have a state-controlled liquor store that employs four persons to dispense alcohol six days a week.

Our choice of regulating our sympathetic and "unsympathetic" nervous system becomes clear. Are we going to be "in control" or are we going to be "therapeutically" controlled?

53

4 – Stress Is Where You Find It

At a recent symposium held on "death and dying," the legal definition of death was considered. When are we alive and when are we dead? One speaker, Dr. Frederick K. Merkel of Rush Presbyterian St. Lukes Medical Center in Chicago, stated: "There is a point in death when there is absolutely no possibility of continued life." That's fine for death but how about life? Is there not a point in *life* when there is absolutely no possibility of continued life unless some drastic changes are made? I've seen too many cases where life didn't continue just because a change wasn't made at the proper time, if at all.

Some excellent research studies recently, show how stress affects our health. One study by Dr. Thomas Holmes in Seattle concerned itself with the relationship of major life events to illness. A large group of patients were asked to rate a variety of major and minor "life events" as to the emotional impact that these events would have on their lives. Each life event was to be rated with a certain number of points. The more points placed on a life event the larger emotional impact it was awarded by the patient. Each patient was given a sheet with 43 major life events listed and included such things as marriage, job change, a family death, moving, conflict with the law, etc. The results are interesting. The top 10 life events, the ones getting the highest points for their emotional impact, are as follows and in this order:

1. death of a spouse
2. divorce
3. marital separation
4. jail term
5. death in the family
6. personal injury or illness
7. marriage
8. being fired from a job
9. marital reconciliation
10. retirement

The medical case histories of this group were then compared with the years in which they reported several major life events. Interestingly enough, illness followed a major life event to a significant degree in this group. Or saying it in simpler terms, stress equals illness.

To me the "top ten" are worth further evaluation. If we start counting, we find that five of the top ten major life upheavels are related to some aspect of marriage. Either death of a spouse, divorce, marital separation, marriage itself or marital reconciliation account for one half of our major life stresses. Now, the solution to this seems obvious, doesn't it, and maybe the "free love" flower children have something going for them. No marriage — no major upheavels and no illnesses.

One flower child insinuated as much to me. She was a plump, straggly-haired Free Spirit 20 years of age who had an aroma characteristic of limburger cheese, gone on. She told me "marriage wasn't for her — she'd seen what it had done to too many of her friends." She then asked me what I thought of "free love." I told her in my most subtle way, that from my casual observation, I felt the price was right.

The top ten may be slightly misleading because "free love" and "living together" isn't up there. The catch is that it wasn't on the list of major life events that the group could choose from. From my office experience I'm sure it would have received a significant number of points. I have found that living together is just great for 16 to 18 months and then the seams begin to open. I wouldn't even know about all these "meaningful" arrangements except that it comes out while I am treating ulcers and colitis and handing out tranquilizers to one or both members of this modern day "Garden of Eden." This isn't my idea, it's the way the charts read. If it's groovy for you at the present time, great. But in my files you're bucking a headwind. As one gal said (at 15 months) "Hell, this is worse than marriage. I've got all of the disadvantages and none of the advantages."

But we can't let marriage off the hook that easy. In my practice I'm sure the results are the same, that some aspect of marriage results in at least 50 percent of patients' stress-related illnesses and I would rate it considerably higher. (To prevent a major life event happening to me I must state that this is a professional opinion not a personal opinion.)

If we take another look at the list, it's even more suggestive. If we remove jail term and job loss, we're really left with marriage, illness or retirement. Most of the problems I see in retirement are related to marriage and with a mind like mine, I have to wonder if marriage isn't related to a few jail terms and a few job firings. (My apologies to you people in jail who got into a fight over the dog and not over your wife or girlfriend, or who robbed a bank for a charity!)

How can marriage get blamed for stress in retirement? I have one lady whose husband is nearing retirement. She tells me that her entire group of friends are "shipping out to sea" the day their husbands retire. I approve. Why? Because the husband is going to have 24 hours a day to show his wife how to shape up the house after 40 years of mismanagement. Turn it around. Suppose the wife retired and went down to the office to "shape things up." There would be office people lined up waiting for a vacant window from which to jump.

So, marriage then must be the bad guy if the research is authentic. There is one ray of hope. If we go back once more and look at the head of the list we can take heart. It's the *loss* of our marriage partner that leads the list — maybe it isn't so bad after all. If your wedding rings are beginning to pinch, hang on, we're saving a chapter to look at marriage and what we can do about it. For now, we're just concerned about its relationship to stress.

So back to stress — what is it? Everyone has his own explanation. Some say it is normal that without stress we can't function. Some call it anxiety and feel we need it to get to work or to win a tennis match. The arguments go on and on because we've had trouble measuring it. We can't weigh it, see it or feel it so it's pretty elusive. Or at least it has been. We're getting closer, though, with some new advances.

Biofeedback is going to be a big help and is already helping many people. What is biofeedback? It sounds complicated but it's very simple. It's the measurement of brain waves, skin temperature and muscle contractions. A pair of sensing electrodes are placed on the forehead, or finger, or at the back of the head and we can monitor functions on a dial or by listening to a tone. The machinery may be complicated but the principle is very simple. Taking your pulse is biofeedback. It's really that simple. It's the measure of a bodily function, your heart rate. Perhaps the simplist and best biofeedback device is a mirror. The lights and beeps on the biofeedback machines are a little more fun and we can measure body functions with considerably more objectivity. We can measure the contractions of the small muscle fiber bundles that make up the larger muscle groups. In a sense, we are measuring the tension in the muscle. If we tighten up our forehead consciously or unconsciously, the beeping gets faster and more intense. If we relax our muscles again, consciously or unconsciously, the beep slows down and gets fainter. The same with the brain's feedback. We can change our brain waves from alpha to beta and vice versa by changing our thoughts. We can warm or cool an area of our skin, and measure it in degrees by altering our thought patterns. This is new and exciting and if you haven't seen or played with a biofeedback machine, do so if you get a chance. It's quite enlightening to see what we can do by "just doing it." We now have people lowering their blood pressure by similar techniques. How do they do it? We don't know! We know the tools they use, the automatic nervous system that we've discussed, but we really don't know how it works.

Because we don't know how biofeedback works, should we hold back, turn off and forget it? We can't afford to. We need all the help we can get to define and treat stress. We used penicillin for years before we knew *how* it worked. We just knew it worked and were glad to have it.

If we're beginning to measure stress, we ought to be able to define it. Webster's dictionary makes it pretty clear:

Stress 1. strain or straining force; specifically, force exerted upon a body that tends to strain or deform its shape.

2. a) mental or physical tensions or strain. b) urgency, pressure, etc. causing this.

Now this isn't too hazy, really. "Mental or physical strain or force exerted upon a body that tends to strain or deform its shape." That narrows it down considerably for all of us. This is the "stuff" that we're talking about. We're not describing the stress required to stay awake, or get up in the morning or play a game, or drive the car. Someone said that all of life is stress and in a sense that's right. If not the case, we'd probably live forever. But again, this isn't what we're talking about. A lot of this is "fun" stress and you and I want our share. We just want to avoid or conquer the stress that "strains or deforms our bodies."

Granted we can turn getting up, playing a game and driving a car into a form of stress that "deforms" and some of us become experts at it, but we have to "do it," it doesn't just occur. It's back to the biofeedback machine. The harder we try to "relax" or "beat" the machine the worse we do. If we just sit back and quit fighting it, think a pleasant thought, "it occurs." We get our autonomic nervous system back on our side where it wants to be!

I've discussed how we can cause all sorts of trouble with our skin, stomach and colon, and can cause fatigue and headaches and even heart problems. I pointed out that we do it by "overriding" our uncontrollable nervous system. But I didn't say how, because no one really knows. It just happens and for now we have to accept it and work on using the principle.

But what kind of person would go around "overriding" his automatic nervous system, and isn't there a place for him in the mental ward?

Speakers are guilty of overriding when their pulse increases thirty percent when they head to the podium.

An asthmatic who is allergic to dust overrides, by having a severe asthmatic attack while watching a movie of a dust storm. An asthmatic that is allergic to flowers can do it when a bouquet of plastic flowers is brought in and provoke a severe asthmatic attack. We had to remove a bouquet of plastic flowers from an asthmatic's room who had a flower allergy, even after we told her that they were artificial. She couldn't control her "overriding."

A patient of mine, who has grand mal epilepsy and who felt a hard seizure coming on while he was walking away from prison to his family waiting outside the gate, "overrode" his autonomic nervous system to his advantage. He told me: "I don't know how I did it. I just couldn't afford to have one at a time like that."

Let's try applying a little stress to a common, if not

glamorous, body function — urination. Now this is a pretty easy one and one we're all relatively skilled at. We know "how to urinate." How do we go about it? We've got to get a lot of things lined up. (Literally.) First, we have to decide to "do it." Then we need to open our urinary sphincters and compress the bladder and we're in business. After we're through all we have to do is close the urinary sphincters and the job is completed. We use our controllable nerves to tighten our abdominal muscles to help exert pressure on the bladder. The opening and closing of the urinary sphincters is all done by the "uncontrollable nerves." If the uncontrollable nerves are truly uncontrollable we're in great shape, we just can't goof it up. But let's go back. Tell me, how did you do it? How did you get the urinary sphincters open and how did you close them at the end? The question is ridiculous. It just happens. All we had to do was to make a decision to urinate and our automatic nervous system was called into play. Our only role was to help out by exerting a little abdominal pressure. After years of practice we have all become proficient and can perform anytime we like. Or can we?

Let's be specific. Suppose you're not reading this but are listening to me in a lecture hall with 200 other people. I ask if all of you know how to urinate and 200 hands go up. Wonderful. That means we've got 200 perfectly healthy normal people present. Now let's assume that I plead ignorance and admit to you that I need help. I suddenly forgot how to urinate and could I please have a volunteer from my mixed audience. I think the experiment would be just as effective whether the audience is mixed or not. I have a receptacle handy. Would someone please step forward and perform so that the group and I might observe?

Now we've applied a small amount of stress or a large amount, depending on your background to the situation. It's really not a life-threatening experience in stress. We're not going to lose our job, wreck our marriage or go to jail or be forced into an early retirement. So, as far as a major life upheaval, we would have to rate it very low. All I'm asking for in my most tactful manner is a chance for all 200 of us to observe you while you perform. How many volunteers would I get? By now, due to the power of suggestion, most of the group would be looking at their watches to see when this mess was ending so that they could get to the restroom and perform in private. Is this the power of suggestion or are we overriding our nervous system again?

I doubt that I would get many volunteers for several reasons. I'm sure that dignity would be reason enough for most. The other reason is quite obvious, it would be hard to perform for an audience. We've "forgotten" how to urinate in five minutes after practicing all our lives. The whole thing sounds a little silly, doesn't it? This automatic function we've done so well without thinking about it has suddenly broken down because some character asks us to perform. If it sounds too silly, think about the last "sample" you had to give at the doctor's office. In our office we wait patiently, for eons it seems, for some patients to urinate. Sound familiar? Many patients have to bring in a urine sample the next day. One healthy fellow recently came in at 11 a.m. and said, "I hope you want a urine sample, 'cause I've been holding it since 4 o'clock yesterday so I would be able to go." He was being awfully considerate of me, but pity his poor bladder!

And how about the hospital setting? People suddenly "forget" after surgery or if they're just in for an illness or diagnostic tests unrelated to the urinary tract. The small army of nurses, doctors, room mates and relatives suddenly become the "audience" and the patient suddenly forgets how to perform a simple body function that he has spent a lifetime perfecting. At this point we try the "hands in hot water technique," the "sitz bath," or that thrill of thrills — the inevitable catheter. There are other causes to be sure such as surgery and medication but quite frequently we just "forget how." What's at work? Nothing's broken, an X-ray would be normal. It's just that we've fouled up our sympathetics and parasympathetics again. We won't "allow it to occur." We have overridden our autonomic nervous system, we have taken control of the uncontrollables to our disadvantage.

I have used urination to show a direct correlation between stress and the body function that we can observe. We can't observe stress at work on the coronary arteries or the stomach or bowel lining but it's the very same principle. We let stress take over the computer and the autonomic nervous system has a new master. The nerves then go to work and constrict the arteries on the heart muscle and cause angina pectoris, or fire up the acid cells in the stomach lining and start inflammation and ulceration, or constrict the small airways in the lung tissues and precipitate an asthmatic attack. We can't afford to miss the correlation. *If we can foul up the autonomic nerves controlling urination in five minutes, we can certainly do the same to our heart or stomach or lungs with days, weeks and months of stress.*

Then why are we so hesitant to accept it? Drs. Friedman and Rosenman have written an enlightening book called *Type A Behavior and Your Heart.* It covers all aspects of heart disease and covers the personality traits of "type A" behavior that they feel lead to coronary heart disease. They feel very strongly that emotions are a large factor and they describe the same frustrations that I have had in getting patients to accept this. The reason patients can't accept it is because most *doctors* won't accept it.

As Drs. Friedman and Rosenman state, "It might seem incredible that very few medical investigators in the past have believed your brain and its function could influence the state of your heart and its own arteries. Yet even now very few cardiac researchers are focusing upon this possible relationship. Even worse, there is still active resistance to this sort of approach. Some investigators indeed have an almost hostile reaction to anyone who dares to 'probe about' in the 'never never land' where mind and body come face to face to communicate with and influence each other.

"Why has there been this prejudice on the part of so many of our colleagues? And, why have so many of our colleagues been even more reluctant to accept as true, or even possibly true, the information brought back to them by those very few who have attempted to invade the many shadowy areas where mind meets body?"

Drs. Friedman and Rosenman's concern about the prejudice on the part of so many of their colleagues is well justified. I have seen one eminent cardiologist after another deride their work as a futility in fiction, or as one cardiologist said, "They would do well to stick with the facts."

We can't stick with facts that we don't have. How many facts do we now have that enable us to prevent coronary artery disease? And, if we have so many facts available why aren't we using them? If we're using them why are we losing so many young and middle aged people with coronary attacks?

Why is it so threatening to see exciting explorations along new and promising frontiers being made? Drs. Friedman and Rosenman feel there are four main reasons why we won't accept stress and the emotional component:

"First, almost all scientists share the desire to measure phenomena and to express such measurements in solid, understandable, and repeatable units — pounds, grams, volts, ergs, degrees of color changes, radioactive emissions and so on.

"A second reason for the failure of past cardiac investigators to study the role of man's personality in the genesis of coronary artery disease is that they lacked knowledge of or interest in the mental or emotional processes of mankind.

"A partial explanation for the persistent hesitation of heart researchers to include man's personality in the ambit of their studies was the inability of most psychiatrists to detect any peculiarity or identifying quirk in the personality of the coronary patient.

"The last point, the positive resistance of the potential coronary patient to visit a psychiatrist, is due, of course, to his absolute confidence in the total integrity of his emotional faculties."

The first three areas of resistance interestingly enough are due to doctors' resistance and only the final one is due to patient resistance. So it's indicative of where the problem lies — with the medical profession, not the patients.

60

At this point I must come to the defense of the coronary patient and join in his resistance. If I am the coronary patient and have "absolute confidence in the total integrity of my emotional faculties" I would prefer not to spend undue time on the psychiatrist's couch having him point out "peculiarities or identifying quirks" in my personality. If I didn't have anginal pain at the beginning of the session, I'm sure I would have it at the end. I would much prefer to hear my family physician or internist explain to me that he was having some doubts about my "absolute confidence in the total integrity of my emotional faculties." And, I would want him to have a twinkle in his eye when he told me so. I personally feel that any physician who has spent enough time with the patient to establish the fact that he has coronary artery disease should be fully aware of any personality traits that could stand modification. The doctor and the patient must then take the time and the effort to establish ways of modifying these troublesome traits. For after all it's not the heart that is killing the personality — it is the personality that is killing the heart.

All of my patients with coronary artery disease lose their resistance to help very quickly and do not need the attention of a "quirk identifier." We can handle the patient's resistance. It's the *doctor's* resistance that concerns me.

I would agree with all four points that Drs. Friedman and Rosenman make and would add one more — the time factor. Every time this comes up in medical circles, the professionals pay lip service to the emotional concept. The final resolution that is always silently and casually passed however is that it's too "time consuming."

Or as one associate put it: "It's not economically feasible to spend the necessary time and besides that's not what the patient came to see me for."

Not economically feasible for whom? And what *did* the patient come in for — to get well!

One member of a cardiac team told me with disgust: "The daily surgery schedule of coronary bypass surgeries absolutely makes me ill. It's become a fad and no one's about to stop it."

Another cardiologist said the same thing in a different manner. "You know — I'm one of the most conservative ones on the whole surgical team."

Why is no one about "to stop it" even though the results are much in debate and we have no evidence that life is being prolonged with bypass surgery? The surgical procedure is much faster and easier to do by far and is certainly more "economically feasible" than helping someone get out of that muddy rut! We are going to be getting better results when we start having patients bypass their old habits rather than bypassing their coronary arteries.

Sylvia's case demonstrates this whole concept. Sylvia is a

52-year-old married woman who came to my office at the end of a long, frustrating ordeal. She was very pleasant in spite of it all and was not basically a neurotic, crock or hypochondriac as she was literally beginning to feel.

She told me that one year ago she developed pain in the lower right portion of her abdomen. She consulted a gynecologist who did a D&C (uterine scraping). The pain persisted and he did a second one and again, no relief. He proposed a third D&C and Sylvia objected. He then referred her to a radiologist who did X-rays of her kidneys. Everything was fine and the radiologist sent her back to the gynecologist. The gynecologist, now in doubt, sent her to an internal diagnostician who did a very thorough workup. He did chest X-rays, upper and lower "GIs," a sigmoidoscopic exam and numerous blood studies. He told her, "I find nothing to explain the pain" and suggested she return to the gynecologist. The gynecologist then referred her to a urologist who hospitalized her and did a cystoscopy and pylecloscopy (placed an instrument in the bladder for a direct look and injected dye up into the ureters and the kidneys). He assured her "all was well" and requested that she see the internal diagnostician once more. She went back and the internist examined her again very thoroughly and repeated the blood chemistries. The internist again explained, "I can't account for your pain on any of my examinations."

The internist referred her back to the gynecologist. The gynecologist determined that Sylvia needed a hysterectomy to relieve the pain. The hysterectomy was done and she was told "there were small fibroids present." One month after the hysterectomy, the pain returned in the right lower quadron where it had been from the beginning. Sylvia was beginning to have doubts and returned to the gynecologist and asked him if a hernia could be present and causing the pain. He examined her and told her that she did indeed have a hernia on the right side and would have to be repaired. He explained to her that he ordinarily did not do hernia repairs but would do so for her. It is interesting to note that neither the internal diagnostician nor the urologist detected the hernia.

After the hernia was "repaired" and healed, the pain was still present in the same area that it had been from the start. She returned to the gynecologist who referred her to a neurologist which Sylvia refused to do.

"They were all beginning to act funny towards me like I was a neurotic or something," she said. "But I'm not. I've never been one to be sick."

Sylvia had 5 hospitalizations, 5 anesthetics and 5 surgical procedures. She had spent a total of $17,000 and still had her original pain to say nothing of the pain incurred along the way.

When I first saw Sylvia she had the pain as before and was

now developing a very severe diarrhea, a colitis in full bloom and was extremely concerned. I asked Sylvia when she had last been well.

"Two years ago I was fine," she answered.

"When did you get sick?" I asked.

"One year ago this month," she replied.

I asked her what she had been doing when she wasn't being examined or operated on.

"Not much," she said. "Just driving up to see mother in the hospital in Washington. I was one of her favorites, you know."

"Oh — what's wrong with mother," I asked.

"It's sad. She's been dying slowly with cancer of the colon the entire past year."

"I'm sorry, where in the bowel did it start," I questioned.

"Right here," she said, pointing to her painful area.

I asked her if any of the other doctors were aware of this.

"No, why should they be?" she said. "It just never came up and what does it have to do with it anyway?"

We discussed the emotional impact of watching her mother die with so much pain and the stress that it could place on her.

"Do you mean — do you think that tension — I can't imagine — and why wouldn't the other doctors have been concerned about it — why would they operate on me if it was tension all along?"

Sylvia was a very intelligent person and showed considerable skepticism to my approach at the beginning. Rightfully so. Needless to say, her faith in the medical profession was totally shattered. She went along with my proposals and we placed her on tranquilizers for a period of two weeks. When she returned the pain was gone and the diarrhea had ceased. Sylvia was beginning to get the picture and she was bitterly angry with her medical care.

She had all of her records sent to me and I reviewed them. The ironic part is that the history and physical sheet that the gynecologist had used had all the body systems stamped on it — heart, lungs, abdomen, nerves etc. Everything had a notation on it except the heading, NERVES. It was completely blank.

"Nerves" — they're too time consuming and not practical to treat. Dr. Hans Selye in his book, STRESS WITHOUT DISTRESS, states: "Similarly many common diseases — peptic ulcers, high blood pressure, nervous breakdown may not be due primarily to such apparent causes such as diet, genetics, or occupational hazards. They may merely be the non-specific stress effects of attempting to endure more than we can. Here, instead of complicated drug therapy, or surgical operations, we can often help ourselves better by identifying the decisive cause which may be a member of our family, or relative."

Stress is where you find it and you can find it anywhere. Relatives and family can cause an intense amount of stress and consequent health problems. I have seen so many people damage their own health worrying about the health of another family member or relative. Husbands and wives, children and their aging parents are both quite capable of this. One of the more common stressful situations I see is what I call the "mother-daughter" syndrome, which is a whole story of its own. (See chapter 5.)

Then there's the new baby syndrome. This will bring dad in with a stomach ache, mother in with a headache and the newborn baby with a worn-out navel. One couple and grandmother brought in a six-week-old baby with a navel that looked like Rudolph's nose. The mother was in tears, dad was in despair, grandmother was in front and center and the baby was in pain. The nurse at the hospital told the new mother to swab the navel four times a day with alcohol. Grandmother wasn't buying new fangled ideas. She told her daughter, "You use olive oil, that's the one thing I do know about babies." The daughter wouldn't buy the olive oil bit and stuck with her alcohol treatment to the navel. Grandmother sneaked behind, wiped off the alcohol, and put on the olive oil. Then mother sneaked behind, wiped off the olive oil and rubbed on the alcohol. The baby's poor navel was getting more rubbing than the abdomen of a Buddhist statue. I tactfully suggested that both the alcohol and olive oil had its place but it wasn't on the navel. I recommended plain water applied gently once a day if time permitted and the navel healed rapidly.

I've often wondered if those happy young student nurses who sit the proud new mother in the wheel chair, plop the baby in her lap, the bouquet of roses in one arm, the formula in the other, and holler, "have FUN" know what kind of practical joke they are playing. Within 24 hours the formula runs out, the roses begin to wilt and mom and dad realize that those "wetting bawls" are breaking up that old gang of theirs.

Unfortunately the problems of child rearing do not end when the navel heals. A considerable number of the health problems I see result from intra-family strife. The stress is a two-way street. I had one 7-year-old girl with actively bleeding ulcers because of a stressful home situation. I can say without qualification that if there is friction in the home, somebody's health is going to pay the price. I have seen numerous divorces occur because the husband and wife cannot agree on a common approach to a teenage problem. Most likely dad cannot stand the length of junior's hair and his lack of responsibility and mother feels it is all right and that father should understand. Or it is a friction between mother and daughter and dad attempts to solve the problem by taking daughter's side. Soon the original conflict is forgotten and the conflict now becomes mother versus dad. I recently watched helplessly as a delightful couple that had been married 27 years get a divorce because of an unresolved argument over their 17-year-old son's hair length.

One of the problems I see is that many of us do things that we really don't approve of. We go ahead and do it anyway because it pays better, or has more prestige, or somebody expects me to do it, or "what would they all think if I don't?" I think we all wear a suit of miniature mirrors, trying to reflect a hundred different views of what we feel a hundred different people want to see in us. One of my patients, a beautician, is a classic example of this:

"I get so tired of changing roles with each customer. This morning I had a school teacher, a prostitute and a preacher's wife," she said. "I have to be an intellectual, a lady of the street, and a saint all within three hours. It just wears me out," she said.

I suggested that she be herself and let her clientele build around that image. Then every customer who chose her would do so because they "approved" of her the way she was and she would not have to be a chameleon. The source of stress is endless as are the threats to our health that it poses. I have noticed that most of the things upsetting us and bringing health problems are usually the small things. We humans do pretty well when the house burns down, or we get flooded out, or the country goes to war. Difficulty comes from the neighbor's dog, the car, the unhappy customer, the boss, the broken appliance on the wrong day, the unnecessary purchase, the traffic ticket, the teacher's comment on the report card, a child's hair length or music — and even the weather.

All too often we deny that stress exists when we are nearly buried by it. I had one lady come into my office with another one of her "splitting headaches" which I felt were tension and had told her so before. She excitedly told me, "Now don't tell me nerves caused this one because I've been downtown shopping all morning for myself and have been having a ball. I'm getting out like you advised, so it can't be nerves this time."

I asked, "Where did you shop?"

"Downtown Portland," she answered.

"Where did you park?" I asked.

"I lucked out, I found a meter, but those damned things. You get a half an hour to shop and it takes you 15 minutes to get to the store. I ran out three times to "feed" it and it was still expired when I got back. Naturally, I had a ticket. It wouldn't be so bad but you can never find a clerk when you want one. When you'd like to be left alone, they swarm all over you. I finally caught one and they were out of my size. I don't see why they run a sale if they don't have half the common sizes. I asked the clerk, why send out sales flyers if you don't have anything? Do you know what she said? 'Better luck next time.' I was so damned mad I stomped out and I'm not going back."

I broke in and said, "You're pounding on my countertop so

hard I'm afraid you're going to chip it."

Her face was tight, her eyes glaring. They gradually faded to an embarrassed smile as she gently pulled her fist back, shrugged her shoulders and saw the humor in the whole blasted mess.

"You were telling me about your fun shopping spree," I said.

We take so much tension and everyday bedlam for a daily way of life that we really don't realize the stress we place on our bodies. I think we have about "adjusted out." Rather than us attempting to further adjust to the bedlam about us we would do better to try to adjust the bedlam.

I had a recent experience that told me how numb we get to the daily pressures and begin to assume they aren't even there. We had a relaxing week in Hawaii. We got off on many of the side roads and were able to enjoy the beautiful, natural splendor of the islands. On my first day back in town, I began my usual freeway trip from the hospital to my office. As cars begin to close in on both sides I caught myself feeling a little shaky. By the time I got to the office I was slightly nauseated. It surprised me enough that I sat at my desk a few moments just thinking about it. The next day was fine, no shakes, no nausea. I had reconditioned myself in 24 hours to accept this pattern and my uncontrollable nervous system had accepted its fate, at least temporarily. How it is really taking it only time will tell!

In the book, *Dairy of Anne Frank,* we see a young girl's reaction to stress from being confined to an apartment during Hitler's tyranny of Germany. Anne could not leave the apartment day or night for fear of being arrested and taken to a concentration camp. I think one of the most interesting insights into human nature is Anne finally risking death to go out into the garden in moonlight to "save my sanity." She felt this overwhelming need to be out in the garden with the flowers and soil, and was willing to risk her life to save her mental well-being.

If you haven't tried nature, you should. Set up a schedule one or two days a week or an afternoon if you can. A walk on the beach, down a country road, along a stream, a mountain trail, a canoe trip — but somewhere away from the roar of society. Remember, stress is where you find it — or lose it.

5 – The Mother-Daughter Syndrome

The mother-daughter syndrome is not listed in the home medical advisor — it isn't there. Don't go to the dictionary — it's not there, either. It isn't a newly discovered medical disorder. You can't even ask your neighbor or doctor about it unless you're ready for a funny stare. It's new. It's my creation — but it isn't really. It's been around as long as mothers and daughters and I'll give full credit to them. If you're a mother or daughter there's a good chance you have it or someday will. Is that good or bad? It all depends on you. Maybe I just hear about the "bad syndromes." They are the ones that make both mother and daughter miserable enough to come see me. It is frequently one of the most destructive relationships I see. So what's it all about?

Let's start by defining a syndrome. I'm a doctor and supposed to know but I looked it up for a crisper definition and to make sure I knew. Blakiston's Medical Dictionary defines a syndrome as "a group of symptoms and signs, which, when considered together, characterize a disease or lesion."

Am I implying that there is something about the mother-daughter relationship that, all things considered, results in a disease? Disease may sound a little dramatic but it's awfully close. I see a lot of daughters (and mothers) with illnesses and showing signs of "dis-ease" due to their relationship.

What age groups of mothers and daughters have "the syndrome"? The older ones. It's not another tale of the rigors of raising children. It's the exact opposite. It's the problem of daughters raising mothers. It appears somewhere in the 25 to 65 year age group for the daughters and in the 45 to 99 year age group for the mothers.

One daughter describes it better than I can. "I have always heard about a girl's being tied to her mother's apron strings but I have a mother who is tied to mine."

Another patient relates it like this: "It's almost like childbirth all over — only this time the umbilical cord is harder to cut because the nourishment is flowing backwards, from child to parent."

Both quotes portray the syndrome, or as we said, "a group of symptoms and signs, which, when considered together, characterize a disease or lesion."

Let's get specific. What are these symptoms and signs and what are they up to? Where do they come from? They're a bag of sick emotions that originate from an unhealthy relationship between two people. They're up to no darn good. Sick emotions, demonstrated by these actual quotes:

"She never calls me — I always have to call her."

"I've given up trying to convince mother that Carl and I are happily married. She objected to the marriage from the start, and nothing will change her mind."

"I hardly know my grandchildren but the way she's raising them it's probably just as well."

"It doesn't bother me that mother can call my brother long distance but can't afford to call me."

"She never smoked while I was raising her."

"Do you know what she did the last time she stayed with us? She took all of my clean sheets and linen out of the closet and took them down and washed them. She told me to never put dirty linens in the closet!"

"If she only knew how sick I am and what the doctor said about my condition maybe she'd act like she cared, even if she doesn't."

"I wanted to go to Omaha to see my children but mother became nauseated the day before and told me she needed me. She says she doesn't know what she'd do if it wasn't for me. My husband wonders if she could be making herself ill each time we want to leave. Is something like that possible, Doctor?"

"I suppose they're going to his parents for the holidays again this year."

"If she would only come over once in a while instead of twice a day. Each time she comes over she tells me something else I'm doing wrong with the two boys."

"Why can't she be more like her sister? Thank God I have one child who cares."

And on and on. These are the things I hear all too often. These are the emotions that begin to surface when I start probing to see why the ulcers or migraines or bouts of colitis hang on despite my medical treatment.

I hear these symptoms from both mother and daughter. I'm in a privileged (or unprivileged) situation. I don't have to take anyone's opinion. I get to formulate my own. It isn't just daughters that come up with the "diseases and lesions." Mother ends up with her share and this further deteriorates a sad relationship. Mother doesn't usually mind her disease. She displays it for all to see and places it on the emotional bargaining table.

One mother, Helen, came to my office directly from her daughter's house and was visibly upset. "I've just been to Janet's house and I know my blood pressure will be up. I get so upset just thinking of going over there. They're just wrecking Raymond, their son, and it just tears me apart inside. He's such a good boy and he's always been my favorite. He practically considers me his mother and we're actually much closer than he and his mother. He confides more in me than he does his own parents. Janet and her husband resent me and always have. I'm certain they feel I'm trying to come between Raymond and them but it's just not so. It's just that they don't understand him like I do. All he wants is love and understanding and they can't seem to see it. He needs room to develop and his father won't give it to him. She and her husband aren't doing so well themselves. They've been on the verge of divorce a few times and if it wasn't for my talking to them they would be divorced by now. It's apparently a 'bedroom' problem and I have told her husband just what I thought about it in so many words. He should have known without my having to tell him anyway — he considers himself a leader in the church."

I sneaked in a blood pressure check during her sermon.

"Well, how is it, Doctor? Don't tell me the numbers if it's too high. I know who caused it. I shouldn't have even stopped by her house today!" (Good chance that Janet would agree!)

"Surprise," I said, "your pressure is normal today, 140/80."

"It can't be! Take it again," she insisted. "It goes up every time I go near her place. She is the cause of its going up in the first place and she knows it."

I checked it again as the easy way out.

"Strange as it seems, it's normal again," I said, "and that's good considering how upset you are. That tells me your pressure is probably staying down most of the time now."

"All right, then," Helen said, "but don't you dare tell her it's normal. Has she called you yet?"

"No, not yet."

"Well, she will, as you know, and whatever you do, don't tell her it's down. She knew my heart was pounding while I was at her house and I told her my pressure would be up for sure. I can always tell when it's getting up there. Just tell her it's not real high and let it go at that. I want her and her husband to both realize that they are the reason for my failing health and maybe they will show me a little consideration."

This type of presentation is a little difficult. I get a similar story but usually it's the daughter who relates it to me. I have never met Janet. I've talked to her on the phone numerous times as she always calls when Helen has been in. She inquires about her mother's blood pressure and health in general and seems very concerned. She has never been critical and is always kind and relieved to know mother is "doing pretty well." Janet has never mentioned a word about the strained relationship she has with mother. She never will unless I ask a direct question. Why? She doesn't want her worst fears to come true. That she truly is the source of mother's health problems. She's feeling guilty enough.

Janet did call shortly after her mother left. She inquired about mother's blood pressure and heart and was relieved to know that her pressure wasn't "real high" and her heart was all right.

Actually, I leaned a little. I told Janet that her mother's blood pressure was excellent and had been for some time. I felt I had to. I had a feeling that Janet's blood pressure was probably higher than mother's. She had every reason to elevate it.

If this isn't the making of a syndrome, a collection of symptoms and signs leading to a physical or emotional illness, it's dangerously close! And as my patient said earlier, "The umbilical cord is definitely harder to cut." It's nearly impossible to cut. It's also most unlike childbirth. When we cut the umbilical cord at childbirth it's a helpful life-giving maneuver. This time it's decidedly different. The nourishment pattern has reversed itself. The vital supply line is flowing faster and carrying a larger load. We're supplying the nourishment to an adult now, not an infant. Severing the cord in this dependent situation will result in an emotional (if not physical) death or deaths, not a new life.

Let's stay with our comparison a little longer. How did we reconnect the umbilical cord to begin with? Or was it ever severed in the mechanical gesture at childbirth? Who's getting any worthwhile nourishment from it and just how life-sustaining is it? If we can't sever it without having an emotional or physical disaster, we've got an awkward setup with two people trying to walk separate paths while bound to each other by an emotional tether. We can answer some of these questions by looking at Helen and Janet's relationship. Who reconnected the life line? Helen did. How and why? As I said, I've never met Janet, but I've taken care of Helen for fifteen years. What makes Helen tick? Very little and that's the problem. Helen is an extremely attractive lady in her late fifties and is very prominent in church affairs. This is a problem Helen can't handle. Helen married her husband to "get out of the house with someone my parents felt could support me." In Helen's mind she had stayed married to Charles for two reasons — "the church and the children." I have seen her on an average of once a month for the last fifteen years, each time with familiar symptoms and an occasional new one showing up. She never fails to repeat a constant theme.

"I would leave him tomorrow if it wasn't for the church and the kids. I should have done it long ago. Actually, I should have never married him in the first place. I never loved him then and I have never learned to love him during all these years. You probably don't understand but it's true. I have never loved him in any way. Why my parents would have pushed me out at 17 years of age with a man 10 years older I will never know, except that it was during hard times and I know they wanted me out of the house. It's just that simple. I've left him for weekends but I always had to come back. I couldn't do it to the children even after they were married. I always told myself I would leave him after the children were gone. I should have. I know that now. I still would but it's too late and now I feel sorry for him. Besides, I don't want to set a bad example for the children to follow."

Who reconnected the umbilical cord? Mother. Helen is miserable and with plenty of reasons. She's got herself an emotional conflict twenty fathoms deep and she's drowning in it. She needs nourishment badly and she's going to get it somewhere. And guess who has been chosen to pick up the tab. It's time someone started repaying a long overdue debt. Mother isn't going to be tactful about presenting the bill. She's already done that, as we've seen. After all, the pregnancies kept the marriage together and "nearly wrecked" Helen's health in addition. That's a monstrous debt to liquidate for either party. It will never be liquidated to mother's satisfaction. The tragic part is that if the pattern follows the usual "syndrome" (and it appears to be) her daughter will fall for the ploy out of guilt and try to do the impossible: to repay the long standing note and add interest to it. How?

Here comes the nourishment mother is so desperately searching for. Nourishment in the form of attention and guilt on Janet's part. Mother is actually reaching for an "emotional out" from her miserable existence. She's treating the wrong illness with the wrong prescription and the result will be as expected — a disaster for two or more people! Helen is facing increasing years with a man "she never cared for." She is acting much like a hyperactive child. She's not going to sit back and take it. Her presence is going to be known and felt by someone, namely her daughter Janet.

Helen has already entered her daughter's marriage. She is trying to emotionally adopt her grandson in a power play between him and his parents. Janet's husband isn't even spared. He can use some advice and he's getting it! I don't know what Janet's health is like but I would venture a guess because I take care of too many "Janets" suffering from the "mother-daughter" syndrome. Remember, the reason I hear about this whole syndrome is because it usually leads to an illness. If Janet isn't troubled now with migraine headaches and fatigue, or a stomach or colon problem she most likely will be in the near future. I hear any or all of these symptoms so often in this situation. Usually my treatment is ineffective because the source of the problem is not approached. I can treat the headaches and fatigue, the stomach and colon problem and get some temporary relief but we're working on the wrong end.

The daughter is generally painfully trapped. She is human herself. She can't, in her analysis, even fight back in her defense. Here's a mother that is nosing into her marriage, who enjoys telling me that her daughter's marriage is rocky at best, who has nearly adopted her daughter's son and who then plays her trump card — failing health. Janet just might be tough enough to stand up and clear the air on mother's intrusion into her life, if mother's health wasn't in jeopardy. But mother's health (according to mother) is in jeopardy and it just may get worse. It certainly will if someone doesn't start paying attention or making waves! Janet is going to accept her mother's version of her health, not mine. Daughters always do, even though I reassured Janet it doesn't help her side much. She really can't accept my assurances of mother's good health after hearing and seeing mother's side. Mother is a better salesperson than I am. She spends two hours handing (and acting) out symptoms and I get a short telephone shot to try to even the score. I'm not very effective. Whose word has meant the most over the years? Whose presence is omnipotent? Mother. Who plans to keep it this way? Mother. She can ill-afford not to, from her vantage point. She's determined to keep the health matter in full view or their whole picture might take a logical turn and that's to be avoided above all.

Someone just might decide that this is sick nourishment indeed and life-sustaining to no one. Janet just might sever the whole emotional binder by a squaring off of sorts. She's the only one who could possibly take the initiative. Janet is trying to nourish mother while she herself is starving. She's starving for a normal relationship with her mother, a tolerable day and freedom from headache, fatigue and a "knot in the stomach."

Can't daughters climb above all this and see it for what is is? Not usually. Mothers are special people and that's the problem. We all have at least one. Maybe daughters could and should meet the challenge but from my experience not many of them do. Incidentally, the first four women that I told about this chapter concerning the "mother-daughter syndrome" all reacted the same.

"Would you like a whole book about it?" one asked. "I could write it for you." She then proceeded to do so. She didn't write a book but she wrote about twenty-five single-spaced pages of a pathetic mother-daughter relationship.

The second one said, "It's about time someone did. It's probably too late for mom and I but I'd love to see it. Maybe we could start fresh."

The third one said, "Oh, I couldn't bear to read that, I just couldn't."

The last one said, "Great! Tell me the title of the book and mother and I will read it together. I promise. I'm sure we both know what a sorry situation we have and that we are fighting a ridiculous tug-of-war. We should really be enjoying each other at this stage but we're not. Not in the least. You won't understand, Doctor, but I love my mother yet I can't stand her. It doesn't make sense, does it?"

It makes a lot of sense. It touches the raw nerve endings we've been talking about. It's the very heart of the problem. Mothers and daughters do love each other. That's why the "syndrome" develops in the first place, because two people care so much. It's the over-caring that sets up the problem.

It's the same with doctors and their families. We may feel that we're the most qualified doctor in the surrounding ten states but we always ask a colleague to do the surgery. Why? Emotions again. We can't treat our wives or children like we would another patient. We care too much. That doesn't mean we don't care about our patients. It's just that we don't "over care" and, more importantly, we don't overreact like we no doubt would if we ran into complications during surgery on a member of our family.

Patients benefit from this mental stance that we take with them even though it may sound insensitive. It's not insensitivity — it's objectivity — and that's what counts when life is at stake and that's what all of us lose all too often when we're dealing with family members. (It's more of the "blood thicker than water" stuff.) That's why we don't usually do too well teaching our children to swim or play the piano. We care too much and try too hard. We all know the usual result.

It's the lack of objectivity that causes the syndrome and maintains it. Mothers and daughters that are locked into this picture I've painted wouldn't think of reacting to their friends as they do to each other. We may give and take with our friends, but if a friend begins to put too much pressure on us or make us uncomfortable we send out some subtle but usually effective messages to them. If things get too bad we call a necessary halt to the relationship. We get to a "take it or leave it" spot. We get to the point where it's easy to "not care."

But, mothers and daughters can't cut off the relationship, and they know it. And I agree. Who wants to cut off anything between mothers and daughters, although I've seen so many situations where it couldn't help but be an improvement in the relationship.

I've seen numerous situations where both mother and daughter take a "to hell with you" attitude. "We're just not going to see each other anymore."

One patient told me, "I gave myself a birthday present today. I called mother and told her off."

It doesn't last long in most cases. Some emotion-laden day comes around such as a birthday or anniversary and they give it another try. It's usually an unnerving day for both and they most likely renew their vows to "stay away from each other." Absence sounds as if it may be the solution but it seldom is. Emotions aren't controlled with a pronouncement.

I see both mothers and daughters in the office for their various health problems and the conversation invariably gets around to the smouldering problem.

I hear things like, "I think I know what's causing my stomach trouble — worry about mom. We never call each other. I feel so guilty about it and yet each time we've gotten together I'm upset for weeks."

Mother says, "I don't know where we went wrong. I did the best I knew how. I treated HER like all the rest. I get along with the rest of my kids. Maybe someday I'll understand. I guess it's best this way."

It's not "best" this way and mother didn't treat HER like all the rest. She only thinks she did. For a number of reasons, unknown to mother or daughter, this relationship was different. It may have been subtle things such as the timing of this daughter's appearance in the family, or her being the "one I could count on," or a somewhat weaker or more sensitive daughter in her formative years. It may have been a change in mother's position in the world such as losing a husband by death or divorce, or simply a different outlook. Whatever the reason, the "treatment" and relationship are different and two people pay an enormous emotional price because of it.

I mentioned before that I frequently ask my patients to write their life story.

Let's look at one of these "life stories" that a 29-year-old patient wrote and see if we can spot any potential mother-daughter syndrome material. Sandra had ulcers and had been losing weight. She did not come in complaining of problems between her and mother, only a stomach ache and an ulcer that would not heal with the usual antacids and diet control. She had lost twenty pounds and they were pounds she couldn't afford to lose. She wrote a long and introspective story about herself at my request.

The following are some sentences taken out of the story and may be slightly out of context but they demonstrate clearly how Sandra was not treated like "all the rest."

"I couldn't stand my relationship with Bob but mother always made me stick with him because a girl needed an escort to go to school social events.

"I tried to break off our relationship in the summer after our senior year but Bob worked for dad and he would have been without a mechanic and good help was hard to find, dad said.

"Before Christmas my mother was bugging me about my periods. I hadn't had two but I knew I couldn't be pregnant. I was. My mother wrote me a letter I will never forget. Bob and I were married. My parents insisted on that. He went to work for my dad full-time.

"I was so ashamed for *mother* but I took the baby to the baby shower they had planned for me.

"Bob and I made weekend trips to Idaho at least twice a month to see my parents. My mother always had Judy, our daughter. Mother convinced me it tired me out to have the baby around all the time. She said I needed time to do things I couldn't do with a baby around. Little did I see the damage that was being done.

"Mother expected us every holiday and birthday.

"After our second daughter was born, mom started suggesting I didn't care for Judy. Dumb me, I let her take her for weeks.

"Dad had his first coronary on Christmas, one of the few holidays we didn't get home. He recovered from his heart attack but had a fatal one two years later on their wedding anniversary, the one other date that we didn't make it home for. (It's interesting, and tragic to note, that dad was in on this syndrome.) I went and stayed with mother for four weeks. She went totally overboard with grief. It was like a show with her.

"Bob was killed in a car wreck the following summer. It was so upsetting because we weren't doing well together at the time he was killed. He had talked of taking me and the children to mother's house and leaving us for good. At the funeral, mother pretended to carry me and whispered, 'Cry! Cry!' Only later, at night when the children were sleeping, could I allow myself to cry.

"We were managing just fine until a year later when mother announced she was moving in with me and the children. I soon learned that if we were to get along my house was no longer my own and eventually my daughters weren't mine either, but I couldn't bring myself to kick her out. She moved back to her home for three months but once again decided she was moving back in with us for good. She resented Carl, a friend I met at work. She told me I was spending more time with him than I was with her and that he shouldn't discipline my children when he came over.

"At Christmas Carl gave me a ring. When I showed mom the ring she exploded and said I was thinking of myself and not her or the children. When I told her we were getting married anyway she explained all the 'hell I had put her through.'

"We planned a small wedding but mother wouldn't hear of it. She planned a bigger one to suit her and her social standing.

"Mother went to live with her mother after the wedding. (Where does the syndrome stop??) She told everyone I had disowned her. I got sick to my stomach every time the phone rang for fear it was my mother calling. The only time she was nice on the phone was when she wanted the children again.

"At this point the children are so confused they don't know what to do. They're behaving terribly and threaten to leave and live with Grammy if I or Carl correct them at all.

"In myself I am very disappointed: as a mother, a wife and a human being. I am supposed to be a mature woman and yet I can't stand on my own judgment. I shy away from relationships for fear

I'm not good enough. Why am I so vulnerable? I don't know unless maybe I robbed myself in growing up. My children don't know how to laugh. I'm afraid I've robbed them of something very precious."

Sandra has truly been robbed, but she didn't rob herself. She has been the victim of an emotional pickpocket, first degree. She hasn't been treated "like all the rest." No one can spend this much time domineering one daughter and have much left to go around. Why was Sandra singled out from her older sister and brother? We don't really know and it doesn't matter much at this time. It's obvious that mother selected the right one to set up the "syndrome." She has totally undermined one daughter's chances for a happy life. The two girls now have definite behavior problems and are failing in school. Judy has been pegged a "hyperactive child" by a psychologist. What else would we expect? The new husband is a real catch but is "unwelcome in mother's home." The real coup for mother is that Sandra feels she's robbed herself! She's disappointed in herself as a mother, a wife and a human being.

Why didn't Sandra see the light? Why doesn't she see it now? Why didn't she take a stand long ago? Maybe it was an early pregnancy. Maybe it can be written off as youth and immaturity. That could be an excuse for Sandra and this case. But youth and immaturity won't explain the next two charts on my desk. One is a case history about Sarah, age 70, and her mother who is 93 and they're still "going to it."

As Sarah states: "I'm trapped into living with a religious fanatic mother who has a quick temper. I've resented her since childhood because she beat me so often and impressed on me how unattractive I was until I became quite withdrawn at age 11. She was selfish and demanding and I'm convinced her blaming my father for my retarded brother caused dad's early death. At 93 she still pouts when I don't knuckle under and shows her disapproval of most of my activities."

The next chart is that of a 46-year-old "daughter" whose hypertension was totally out of control due to her worrying over mother's drinking problem. Mother would get drunk and the neighbors would call Carol, her daughter, to come and stay with her. Mother lived seventy miles away and this was happening so frequently that Carol was a nervous wreck. I finally convinced Carol to write mother and tell her she would have to make it on her own until we got Carol's blood pressure under control.

Carol brought me the letter to show me she had followed my request. I read it and realized once more how impossible it is to be objective with mothers. It was a delightful letter, nearly begging in tone. Carol pleaded with mother to please understand and asking her to "please not think less of me." All she really asked for was a "month off" from her daughterly duties so she could regain her own health. Carol was so apologetic you would have thought she was ordering mother's demise! She concluded by saying, "I realize, Mom, that I'm asking you to have great faith and understanding but you must let go and trust me."

This would be sad enough but Al, her husband, clinched it. He felt obligated to add a letter of his own with a similar pleading tone. He concluded his letter by saying, "This is asking a **great, great** amount of understanding and faith of you, Mom. Please know we love you and share with us our convictions that it was necessary to dissolve the dependent relationship which exists between you and Carol for now. Once this has been done a more meaningful life will emerge."

If it's hard for a mature, intelligent couple to temporarily sever a few ties, we can excuse Sandra and all the other daughters for feeling as though they have "robbed themselves."

I have one 66-year-old lady who asked for an excuse from me to show mother stating her "blood pressure was elevated and she couldn't visit her every day until it came down." I wrote it for her, in total disbelief. The patient showed my brief note to her mother, and guess what? Mother went into a rage and advised her to change doctors immediately. No shyness on mother's part!

Another mother, aged 70 and a patient of mine, handled her "problem" differently. She went to bed and refused to eat. The daughter called me and said that the mother was in a terrible depression and was getting weaker by the day. I asked them to bring her into the office, which they were able to do only after considerable persuasion.

"What's the matter, Martha?" I asked. "I hear you are staying in bed and not eating."

"That's right, Doctor. I'm so weak. I know what the problem is and so do you. You take care of my daughter, and you know she doesn't care about me."

I did know her daughter, and such was not the case. So I questioned her thoughts. Martha responded:

"Oh, she tries in her own way. She calls every day and we talk for half an hour and she comes over three afternoons a week to see me, but it's obvious she doesn't have time for me any more."

Mothers and daughters must be unsavory characters if any or all of this is true. You and I know better. Mothers and daughters are special people and deserve an appropriate relationship, a relationship that flourishes as well as nourishes in both directions. It should have enough quality to be treasured above any family heirloom. In essence, it is a family heirloom and will be passed on to future mothers and daughters, whatever forms it takes. It is a relationship so deeply emotionally rooted that every other relationship that mothers or daughters enter into will be affected by it. Husbands, children and friends all stand to either gain or lose, depending on the nature of the relationship. We can't forget it, call it off or pretend the emotions never existed no more than we can cancel the emotions of a previous marriage or a loved one. There has been an emotional commitment made, an investment in time if nothing else, and we can't dissolve it with a verbal or written statement. There's a cliche that states, "Out of sight − out of mind." I'll go along with that but I won't buy, "Out of sight − out of heart."

Death doesn't even solve it. This was brought out so clearly recently when a patient of mine in her late 40's came in totally upset. She had been out of town to her mother's funeral.

She told me, "I'm never going back. I never want to see any of my family again. We spent the entire night before the funeral arguing over who was to get mother's antique lamp. My brother and sister actually came to blows. The conversation finally turned to a heated discussion of who mom liked best. I couldn't believe it!"

What can we do to prevent this syndrome or to improve it once we've slipped into it? Plenty. Mother is in the best position to prevent it. She's the "big girl." She must understand that daughters are to be their own agents. She must see that her ultimate happiness, as well as daughters, rests on a delicate balance of total independence of two people. Total independence, that's the key! It's the same with any other friend you plan to keep. Being "good friends" may sound a little cool but I don't think so. It's really the most we can hope for and a supreme compliment if we achieve it.

A few mothers and daughters do achieve this "good friends relationship." I have one 85-year-old mother patient with four daughters who we could use as a model. It is not a syndrome, but a marvelous relationship that is a joy to see and feel. The beauty of this relationship is extended to the daughters' husbands and all the grandchildren. The husbands are all the type that I would choose for a lifeboat partner. They can't do enough for their mother-in-law, not because they have to, but because her daily existence deserves it. The grandchildren adore her, and are the type that take time out of their busy schedules at college to write me a thank you note for getting her over some illness. I see lots of love flowing in all directions, with "no strings attached" and no favorites. I see an occasional difference of opinion between mother and daughters, with understanding on both sides. I see lots of joking and teasing back and forth to keep each other in line, and both mother and daughters benefit from it. I see an occasional disappointment, but no guilt reactions. It is a relationship that is a true heirloom.

The natural tendency is for mother to "hang on to her daughter." I've found a tendency in some daughters to bask in this spotlight while they complain about it. Mother and daughter have to realize that there is a time when this dependent relationship has to end or it will progress into the sick relationship I've been describing. This is a hard step for mother to take, especially so if she is unhappy, or alone (or both), and approaching her later years. Yet this is the very path that she must take if she is to find any true happiness.

I spent most of a recent weekend at the hospital trying to save the life of a 59-year-old "daughter" who died with acute alcoholism. She had moved in with mother twenty years ago to care for her. She spent her days drinking sherry out of pure frustration. She paid the ultimate price of the syndrome, a fatal collection of symptoms and lesions. Mother is just as healthy as she was twenty years ago. Has she found happiness?

We can compare the situation to a cruise ship. Mother sees her life as a lonely inactive existence. She feels out of the mainstream and senses a void. She sees her children and their families embarking on a life-long, fun-filled voyage. She's not going to be left behind standing on the dock when the ship pulls out. She's going to find a deck chair for herself and partake in all the festivities. If mother adds to the fun and merriment of the cruise, like any other passenger, all is well and as it should be. The problems arise when mother approaches the bridge of the ship and begins to take over at the helm. At this point, daughter's position changes and she is assigned the job of ship's steward: to see that the captain and all the passengers have every whim and need taken care of. The end result is that the ship soon strikes an emotional reef and a tidal wave of tears and guilt engulfs all hands. Happiness harbor is never reached. As an old saying goes, "A good crew is a ship's true treasure."

This is why so many daughters tell me, "I can't understand it. I get along better with my mother-in-law than I do my own mother." Mothers-in-law, despite the jokes, can be more objective. They're more content to be another passenger on the cruise, or at least a silent captain.

Daughters must diagnose the problem in an objective fashion. This is hard, and as we've seen, nearly impossible sometimes. As we said, objectivity doesn't come easy. The first step is to get some buried emotions uncovered. How did the syndrome start? When did it start? How and why do we keep it going? Discuss the relationship with mother and let her know your feelings. Neither of you are mind readers. Once we see the problem and once we accept it for what it is, then we can change it. It's a starting point.

Get down to specifics. Leave the promises and guilt, the love and indebtedness out of it for now. Talk about the problem that exists today. Is it a problem of time and busy schedules on daughter's side? With a husband and children it very often is. Decide between you how much time you have for each other today, this week or this month. If you don't have time for two visits or two phone calls a day, decide how many you would enjoy. How often do you enjoy seeing and talking to your best friend or friends? That should be a good gauge. Limit your time and each meeting will be more meaningful to each of you. It may sound selfish but it's not. The height of selfishness is spending time together that you can't afford to spend. That's forced giving and that's the definition of selfishness. You can appreciate each other's opinion, but that's all it is, not a blueprint for life. If the subtleties don't bear fruit you'll have to bear down until they do.

It may sound like a calloused approach, but it's not. Our goal, remember, is to improve a relationship, not destroy one. There's a big difference. You shouldn't be guilt-ridden for taking a stand. The guilt should come from doing nothing and allowing a bad condition to get worse. It takes some brave positive steps and the sooner you take them the better the results. I see so many daughters that wait for a tragic or terminal illness to hit before they develop a "closeness with mother that I never had before."

I don't see the "mother-son" syndrome so often but it does occur. I'm not sure why. Sons, by their very nature, seem to grasp their independence with a firmer hand. A colleague of mine, a surgeon in his late fifties, spends the entire night before mother comes to visit removing all ash trays, cigarettes and alcohol, and "airing out the house."

Mothers aren't always the "bad guys." There is another syndrome along the same theme. It's the "daughter-mother" syndrome and it's just as destructive. It's the complete opposite. Daughter comes home to mother after the divorce with three children for mother to raise. But that's another story.

Remember, the sooner the problem is faced the more happiness there is to find. It it's too late for this "mother-daughter" syndrome there's still work to be done. You have daughters of your own. History doesn't **have** to repeat itself!

6 – The Marriage Go Round

A friend of mine has a full time job teaching school but has a lot of interest and skill in photography. He has decided to try and perfect his skills and help justify his expensive cameras and equipment to his wife (see how marriage can wreck your health?) by taking wedding pictures in his spare time. He does nice work and his pictures are unique and beautiful with intentional double exposures, etc. They invariably capture the mood of the day and most of his "shots" are eagerly purchased by the newly married couple.

He had been concerned lately however because he has worked for a professional studio and he receives a percentage of the amount paid for his pictures that are purchased by the married couple. He was not paid at all for several of the last weddings and he was understandably confused. He was concerned at first that his pictures were unsatisfactory and were not selling, yet he knew better. Then he felt maybe .he was being mistreated by the firm and just not getting his money so he called the studio owner to check into the matter.

He was told that his pictures were fine, that wasn't the problem. It was all very simple. Several of the last few marriages were being "dissolved" before the couple could come in to look at the proofs. Now that's *really moving* in my book. I hate to assume a "holier than thou" stance but I can't help but hold these fast movers in scorn. Especially since I never even thought of dissolving our marriage until Carolyn, my wife, had made me sit through about three showings of our "conjugal catalogue" to various friends and relatives. But we had been married for days by then and that's different.

Seriously, though, when we start dissolving marriages before the pictures of the happy day are developed, I have to wonder if an adequate time was truly allowed to work problems out, or even start them. I hate to sound old fashioned but I also hate to see us resort to "instant print cameras," capable of delivering prints the day of the wedding to keep photography studios from going broke.

Maybe we should hold these fast-dissolving marriages in awe, rather than in scorn. It's possible they're just smarter and able to reach decisions quicker than the other million couples that followed right behind in 1975. A recent newspaper headline told the story, "Annual Split Hits Million." The article related that "the number of divorces in America in one year passed the one-million mark for the first time in history in the mid-70's, according to the National Center for Health Statistics." That's more than double the 479,000 divorces recorded in 1965. How can we account for this? One logical explanation would be a larger population and hence more marriages with consequently more divorces. However, the center also reported that the national marriage rate has been dropping about four percent at a time when the number of Americans of marriageable age is increasing. That makes the figure doubly impressive.

Now regardless of how you and I feel about these facts, we at least have to assume something is at work here. Something is causing the divorce rate to skyrocket from 500,000 to one million in 10 years at the same time that the marriage rate is going down.

The data gets even more confusing. A survey of high school seniors of a recent graduating class reveals that 89 percent of the students who plan to marry favor a legal marriage contract. Nothing seems to add up. The only logical explanation would be that we're graduating students who can't read the newspaper, but I doubt that. Yet the facts are much like saying we are having twice as many commercial plane crashes and fatalities during a time when the total number of commercial flights has been reduced — and still 89 percent of the potential future travelers prefer flying to any other mode of travel. Let's start digging a little.

We have decided that marriage, or some aspect of it, causes more major life upheavals followed by illness than any other life event. One million couples then improved their health prospects last year by eliminating marriage. We had better go back to our top ten major life upheavals, though, because divorce is one aspect of marriage. We find divorce in the number two spot, or second only to the loss of a spouse as a major life upheaval. So, one million couples or two million people have actually subjected themselves to the second largest major upheaval in life available and that's not healthy at all.

Why is marriage and all of its related fallout such a health threat? For one thing, it's something most people do. (As of this writing.) And if most of the population marries then we're going to lose husbands and wives, either by death, separation or divorce. If we separate or divorce, we may try reconciliation and that's still more dangerous than retirement in the "top ten" stress rating. Or worse yet we lose partners for all practical purposes but continue to "share shingles" for the next fifty years. I think this may be the biggest health hazard of all. I have seen some marriages stick together as some sort of "mutual revenge" pact, and these make divorce look like a blessing! One case comes to mind:

A patient came in upset and asked me for some tranquilizers because she and her husband were planning a golden wedding anniversary celebration for her husband's parents. Plans were going well until the older couple, Jake and Sarah, heard about it.

82

Jake literally flipped. He telephoned his son and started shouting, "What's going on? If you're planning a celebration for us, you'd damn well better stop it right now, do you hear?

"If you think I want to celebrate 50 years of warfare with her, you're crazy. Here's your mother."

Mother confirmed it, "That's right! You know better — what do you think we should celebrate? Now, you cancel it. We won't hear of such a thing!" Jake and Sarah were dead serious. They were upset that someone would even think of celebrating their past 50 years. The party was called off and the son and daughter-in-law were upset and felt cheated.

The thing that sets this marriage apart is the outspoken hostility and the years they've spent at it. The ones with unspoken hostility (the garden variety) are worse yet. If we're going to live like this, I'll cast my vote with those who reconsider while their pictures are still being developed at the studio. We said, remember, the longer we stay in our old muddy rut, the bigger the health hazard and the harder it is to "get out" without a major disaster.

Someone said, "A successful marriage is one in which hostility has become a habit." Common perhaps — successful, no.

We've been circling the problem long enough and it's time to follow some of the "spokes" to the center and see what's at the "hub" of the problem. Too often we tend to pick out one "spoke" of the marriage wheel and say this is the reason the marriage is rolling along a little bit bumpy, or this is the "spoke" that has to be right to make the marriage run smoothly. It's usually the sexual spoke, and we spend all our time trying to fit all the shattered pieces of this spoke together. It's a little absurd. We know that on any wheel all the spokes play an equally important part. Looking at the spokes makes sense and could be part of an important maintenance program. The problem is, when we examine a spoke we never follow it centrally; we always tend to follow it away from the hub and away from the real problem. We don't stop until we hit the well-worn rim and then have one of two choices. We can stay on the rim and continue going in a vicious circle, or discard the wheel and say it wasn't meant to roll smoothly anyway. I don't like either one of these options we're left with and neither do you.

Our only real hope, then, to improve the situation is to follow the spoke towards the hub. All too often, though, only one member of the marriage is willing to make this examination. One of the brave marriage partners comes in and bares his or her soul and that's a beginning. When I explain that it takes two people to solve two people's problems, I get the usual answer: "he or she" won't come in. "I'm doing fine. If *you've* got a problem, go get help, but don't bug me."

We get nowhere of course. Each partner must be able to

examine the problem or we're wasting time. The ones that do work together frequently don't see the "hub" as it really is. People tend to take different viewpoints; it's like one examining the wheel from the top carriage seat while the other one is on the ground looking up.

The remaining stumbling block if we don't have enough is that when both see the problem as it really is, they often don't like what they see. A solution usually means one or most likely both people have to be willing to change some feelings and actions. It's what one of my friends calls "CIC" or cancel if close. He plays the futures market and will put in an offer to buy a commodity well below the current selling price. If it drops this far, he feels it's a buy. When it begins to drop and approaches his offer, he begins to wonder if the market is trying to tell him something that he is not ready to face, that it may keep on going down. So he tells his broker "cancel the order if close." Too often we "cancel if close" if we can't accept the challenge of change. We can't get out of our ruts, as I've said, by just wiggling the handlebars. We can't apply lip service only or seek help from outside professionals with our minds already made up. This is one reason most marriage counseling fails miserably. One or both parties are grudgingly going along with counseling for at least one or two sessions as sort of an emotional balm; after the separation or divorce we can at least say, "I tried, but it was just not meant to be."

The last possible option is to tolerate the marriage and "do our thing." This takes numerous paths. We can get interested in others or other things and it works equally lousy for husband or wife. We can find our perfect secret lover or we can bury ourselves in hobbies, work, civic or social affairs, charity work or going back to college. All these efforts have about the same efficiency and the same results. I'm not belittling all these attempts at help; they just don't work. It's like trying to solve our problems from the outside in.

It always amazes me the time and effort people will put in studying Mandarin Chinese, or on meetings and committee work, or volunteer services to tolerate the problem when a well-spent ten minutes a day would usually solve it.

It reminds me of a patient who had taken the "cure" at one of the alcoholic centers. He wrote them a letter telling them he was confident his drinking problem was cured, but that it should be mentioned to the other patients that "marijuana is a fine, harmless substitute for alcohol." It's a substitution, not a solution.

Marriage has been around for a few thousand years. Numerous arrangements have been tried and are being tried to replace it. The competition seems to be getting a little more plentiful and more vocal but from what I've seen of their products in my files, I don't see marriage as an endangered species.

Walk into the bookstore and head for the "Marriage Section" and look at all the titles suggesting new and exciting types of marriages. Don't try this on your luncheon hour because you won't get through the first of the ten shelves. I know, because I've tried!

I have read a good many of these books and they have some excellent ideas. Ironically, most of the ideas they propose for the new "casual or open" marriages, would work beautifully for the "closed marriages." (Some of the things they propose would be more useful as a breeding manual for mink farmers!)

We rapidly forget that we got married in the first place to *ENJOY* each other more often than once or twice a week when we could arrange it. That's about the only reason I see that makes any sense out of marriage.

I have a little off-beat approach I use with a couple when they come in with marital troubles. Rather than asking what has brought them to the brink of separation or divorce, I ask, "Why stay married?" This usually brings a faint nervous chuckle from both of them and that's about all I get. It's a different approach and they aren't prepared to list all the reasons for staying married. It's not as ridiculous as it seems. I have asked myself frequently after couples left — WHY are they considering staying together and HOW can they stand it?

Time drags slowly and the silence is disturbing. I usually break the silence with a little suggestion. I explain that before they give me any reasons, let me explain the reasons I am frequently given but have trouble accepting.

"Don't tell me you're going to stay married for the children. We've got enough confused kids now. The children will do better with a divorce or separation than living in an atmosphere of continued marital discord.

"Secondly, don't tell me you need the marriage for security. Prisons are secure and just about as inviting. Toss a brick through the bank window and crawl in and you'll be kept warm, fed and clothed at the state penal institution indefinitely. That's security!"

And finally, "Please don't tell me you're staying married for sexual benefits. If you can't find 'true love' in fifteen minutes in any city or township in this country, you're on the wrong side of the street."

I'm dead serious about all three and these are the reasons I used to get. I have recommended that families dissolve the marriage for the children's sake. Security just isn't a legitimate reason. You don't have it anyway if that's what's holding the marriage together, because the marriage won't last. You'd really be better to start making your own security now than being left insecure when somebody pulls the plug. And you'll have to agree, anyone who feels they have to stay married to be assured of sexual attention has been hibernating for the last 10 years!

I keep on waiting and usually one or the other will say, "I suppose because we love each other." Now that's the first time that has come up, and I point it out. The complaints they dropped on me the first 20 minutes didn't sound much like love!

I then tell them love is a little misty to me and I'd like something I can get a clear picture of. It's too hard to define, rather vague, and volumes have been written about it to try and explain it. I tell them it bothers me to try and patch up a marriage using one word, especially one that's as sticky as this one.

By now they're beginning to wonder whose side I'm on. Maybe I'm engaged in fee-splitting with a divorce attorney.

I finally ask if I can suggest a reason and they nervously agree and listen carefully because they are beginning to wonder if there *is* a legitimate reason to stay married.

I've got one reason and only one, and it is distilled from the successful marriages I've seen in my practice, and from my own marriage, which was still successful when I left home this morning.

The only reason for any two people to stay married is so that each day will be more pleasant and purposeful by being together than it could possibly be if they were apart. As we go along, I refer to the above statement as "the principle" and we all three know what we're talking about instead of repeating the whole thing each time, although we do review it a few times just to freshen up our memory. It's amazingly simple but it works miracles. I've seen couples, years later, who have put things back together, just laugh and say, "We're still using the principle — but it just comes naturally now."

Sometimes one or both of the couple will take exception as we go along.

One wife said, "How can I try to make his day more pleasant if he's screaming at me before I get out of bed?" She can't and I don't expect her to, but it's not the *principle* that failed. He didn't apply it. He can't make her day more pleasant by starting it off like that. You can't apply any "ifs or buts." You have to both accept and apply the principle or it just won't work.

Try it tomorrow and watch the wrinkles begin to smooth out. Remember though, no conditions have been added. You have to go the whole route and you should want to. Can you think of one marriage problem that this won't help? If you can't go the whole day, start with a few minutes. That alone can do wonders. Once you start, the minutes begin to flow into hours, days and years. It doesn't hurt to remind yourself each day and the rewards make it all worthwhile.

How am I usually notified of marital problems? The control panel of the patient starts lighting up again. Remember the symptoms: headaches, weakness and fatigue, stomach and bowel problems and nervous skin rashes. Most people, including doctors, prefer to show the world that their failing marriage is one big success. It's like not being strong enough or smart enough to control our fate, as we mentioned earlier. But most of us are lousy actors even when we try. It's my job to try to find the cause of the symptoms, not just treat them, and by now we know where the symptoms usually lead — to some aspect of marriage.

Once the lid is off and the marital problems are brought out, they frequently relate to the bedroom.

"Something's wrong with our sex life."

It sure is! It's probably non-existent. The husband and wife are both rightfully concerned. This is an easy place to take the obvious but incorrect trail. What are sexual problems? They're just more flashing lights or symptoms on the control panel, and we can't treat symptoms or we're lost. Symptoms of what? Symptoms of a poor marriage getting worse. Hang on to your human sexuality manuals but I have never seen a sexual problem that stood alone. Sexual *symptoms* — yes — hundreds of them, but not sexual *problems*. I know that there are a few mixed genes and hormones and bona fide sexual conflicts because of them. But these are the rare cases. I've seen two in 20 years of practice and that wouldn't keep many sexual clinics in business — which might be just as well. One of the members of a large clinic says there are some 20,000 sexual clinics in this country and nearly all of them are "frauds" except for a very few. This bothered me. Since these associations for the advancement of amorous acrobatics have only arisen in the past seven or eight years, how can he possibly adequately evaluate the thousands that exist. If he hasn't spent considerable time at each of them, how can he judge. If he's willing to judge nearly all of them as frauds without any way of knowing first hand, I think he's telling us something about his own. And I agree with him.

If we have 20,000 sexual clinics in this country as has been estimated, and if they only treated 50 people a week, we'd be curing 100,000 problems a week across the country and in 10 weeks we could potentially save a million marriages. That's providing that sexual problems are the root of the problem as we are being led to believe by every magazine, newspaper and wandering "sexpert" in the land. The troublesome point is while these "climacteric clinics" have been growing like thistles over the past ten years, the divorce rate has doubled. In other words, we've yet to see any dividends and I'm not holding my breath while waiting. Maybe most people can't afford the expense even though I recently read that the Internal Revenue Service will allow up to a $5,000 deduction to attend one of these clinics. With the vast amount of material being offered to us on television, the press, magazines and the local book stores along similar lines we can probably save the money anyway. A week never goes by without my receiving some fancy brochure advertising an expensive but scintillating sexual seminar in one of the major cities of this country. I received one brochure advertising a sexual seminar near Disneyland. It was to be a family affair, and the flyer even advertised a "boys and girls" hour for the children. It suggested the children come to "discuss things" without parental interference. That should be easy. Our family has made two trips to Disneyland. Thank goodness our gals spent all their time with Mickey Mouse and the other exciting features there.

The last brochure I received was from one of our local hospitals. The material stated that the seminar would be even more "meaningful" if those attending would bring a "significant someone." A significant someone? Is that as close as we come in our search for a meaningful day? Seminar titles are always provocative but the attendance fee is always prohibitive. It hits me a bit unusual that the usual medical conference fee is between $150 and $200 for a three to five day seminar. The glossy brochures extolling the virtues of the sexual seminar invariably show a price tag of $500 to $1500. To me it smacks a little of commercialism, but I suppose if we're going to become a sexual therapy expert in a few short days, the initiation fee must indeed be adequate for the title gained.

I know I'm taking a hard line here, but I feel I have to. This point of view is not being stated these days. Again, look at the "Marriage Section" in the book store. The titles on eight out of ten of these suggest that a new "physical approach" will put new life in the marriage. It won't. I've seen it tried too often.

I've had too many patients try and fail. They come in with the latest "cookbook for physical love — a thousand new recipes." They have certain pages marked and ask, "What do you think of that!" I've even had newlyweds call on their honeymoon: "We're on page 122 and confused." My advice, "Just walk the beach hand in hand for a start tonight and throw all the 'cookbooks' in a garbage chute on the way down."

I've had elderly people come in who have been happy, they thought, for years. Now they're confused after reading an article or, as one lady said, "Doctor, how could we have done things so wrong all these years?" They couldn't and they didn't! The emphatic point that I would make is that the physical side of marriage is but another important spoke on the whole "marriage wheel." But if we've got ten or fifteen broken spokes in the wheel, we can't concentrate our time and effort finding all the missing pieces of one "shattered" spoke.

Dr. Robert L. Dickinson, a pioneer physician in sex research, promoted the concept that, "All search for the good life is tied to the search for the good in sex life."

My office records say it considerably different. The records tend to say, "Searching for the good life can easily be 'hand tied' by the search for the good sex life," and that's the current path we're on.

I have one very attractive patient, a divorcee in her middle twenties, who is miserable in her search for the "good life."

She told me, "This sex business has gotten to be one big bore. I've really had it with the whole thing. Everyone says that swinging is supposed to be a ball, but it's not. I've lost all interest in sex. I could care less if I ever hear the word again. Besides, how can you swing when you're all swung out?"

A psychiatrist on the "lecture tour" told a group of physicians, "The trouble that begins in the bedroom will often spread rapidly throughout the house." Again, my records say just the opposite. "The trouble that arises throughout the house rapidly spreads to the bedroom." I'm not dreaming; this is what the charts say.

Think about it a minute in your own marriage. What is emotional and physical warmth anyway; it's a state of mind, isn't it? As I've often told patients, the only "sex organs" I know of are between the ears.

Or as many men and women have said, "I can't be treated like a dog all day and be a tiger all night." You and I have to agree if we think back at our last disaster in the bedroom that we've all had. It started hours, days or even years ago. I have yet to see one case of impotence due to a broken bone or one missing orgasm due to an anatomical defect. Organic causes can occur but they're mighty rare! A study is currently being done on impotence in Europe. Twenty patients and 40 cadavers are being studied to see if arterial obstruction to the genitals is a cause of impotence. I'm glad to see the majority of the "cases" are cadavers and will be curious to see the results. I think the cadavers will have an equal or better response than the "living" control group.

Putting all this emphasis on sex in marriage is self-defeating. To say that a marriage is great except in this one area is like describing a pumpkin pie as great except for one piece. You've either got a good pie or a lousy one, and that's the way it is in a marriage, too.

One couple's case demonstrates what I am saying. The couple is in their mid-forties and the wife was in upset because her husband showed no "interest in her." "I can't understand it," she said. "I'm afraid he has an affair going or something because he doesn't even try, and if he does at my request, he's unsuccessful. It's really got me beside myself." She's very concerned and she denies any other conflict at home to account for it.

Later on her husband came in, without their even talking

about the problem and gave me the same story.

"Doctor, I need some help, or we need some help. Evelyn is upset with our love making and so am I. She feels I don't love her and am not interested in her, but that's not so. I've always loved her deeply and still do. But maybe she's right in a way. I'm impotent and she's driven it out of me, that's all, and she's not even aware of it."

"How's that?" I asked, "Can you give me an example?"

"Sure," he said, "it's just like the last time we tried. She had wanted me to fix the faucet and I had promised her I would but I had had a busy week and hadn't gotten it done. She got mad at me and that's okay, but when she said, 'I knew you wouldn't do it. You're just like the rest of your family — you never have been responsible and you probably never will be' — that did it. She wasn't feeling good and I could overlook her being disgusted, but the 'responsible' bit just did it. She felt guilty and wanted to 'make up' later but I just couldn't with her statement going through my mind."

Why has all the attention turned to the physical side of marriage? Because that's the first *symptom* of an ailing marriage. Let's take a look at an unhappy marriage and look in on a typical family upset. Forget the cause whether finances, child rearing, *your* friends and relatives, faulty plumbing, alcohol or whatever. We've got a dispute going and two unhappy people have got to choose their weapons. The choice of weapons for the fight may sound complicated, but actually is very limited. What choice do we have, really? We can't burn the house down, everyone's fanny will freeze; we can't beat each other up (I know, I know) black eyes are hard to explain; we can't adopt the kids out without considerable involvement; and we can't put the friends and relatives "away." The weapon choice has narrowed down to about two things — finances and much more important, our emotional and physical warmth. Financial weapons don't really work too well although separate bank accounts, limiting the wife's mad money, or the wife showing "him" by spending it as fast as he makes it do get tried.

The emotional and physical warmth weapons really work for me and my patients. What makes it so effective? Two opponents can't really "fight" until they get in the center of the ring. Their punches aren't very effective in their separate corners. How much closer can we get than in emotional and physical embrace? This is the center of the ring. Maybe we should rename these weapons and call them the weapons of "no response, lack of interest, something's gone, lack of fulfillment, we just don't have it anymore." It's all the same. We have this whole sack of problems that have been accumulating over the past days and weeks and possibly years and finally the sack begins to split right in the bedroom, and what do we do? We start the next day with the same old sack and add the final problem to it — sex. So, when the bottom falls out of the sack and we look at the heap of problems on the floor, what do we see first? The "sexual problem," right at the top of the pile because it's a big problem and was the last to be added.

If it ends up on top, it's natural that we see it first even though it was added last. That's why the wrong trail has been so obvious and inviting, but unrewarding.

One marriage authority has prospective couples come in for weeks before the marriage so that the partners can be helped to anatomically explore each other to "see what turns them on," the theory being the more anatomically oriented, the more successful the marriage. I'm all for a knowledge of our bodies, but does this hold marriages together? Who knows the human anatomy better than the medical profession, doctors and nurses, and yet we seem to have greater than our share of unhappy and broken marriages.

What is the cause of all our unhappy marriages and divorces? A panel of marriage experts felt that there are four main reasons for our record number of divorces. They list them as follows:
1. A demand today for instant happiness
2. Women's changing status
3. A generation of "love starved" teenagers
4. "Doing your own thing"

Dr. Urie Bronfenbrenner, a professor of psychology at Cornell University, said, "The commitment for one human being for another is being worn away. No one talks anymore about how much fun it is to bring up a child. Single life looks more appealing than marriage. The single parent is being glorified. More and more, divorce seems attractive. Our goal is self-satisfaction and 'doing our own thing.' Living in a family is too much of a hassle and the family unit is being fragmented as a result."

Divorce may seem more attractive, but is it? I've always been fascinated with the "glow" a good number of my elderly patients have. Life seems a breeze and they continue to live each day to the fullest. I've asked hundreds of these people, "What's your secret to an obviously happy life? I need to know, because I'm getting older each day." The first few answers years ago rather shocked me. They don't anymore. They're all the same. What would you guess? Cover the page and don't read on for a few moments while you reflect on the question. It's not what we would expect, not security, not material possessions or fame, not successful children or the proper clubs and social standing. "A long and happy marriage," they invariably reply. This applies whether or not they are alone now. I think it's fascinating and helpful. If this is their secret, we should know and that makes working out some problems a bit more urgent.

Robert Browning said, "Grow old along with me! The best is yet to be." Maybe that's what he was getting at.

I recently asked a 71-year-old man who was in for a physical how long he had been married.

"Forty-five years, doctor, and it's all been swell. We've had our ups and downs but it's been great as I look back. Early in the marriage we had hard times and I had to go on relief. She was right there with me all the time and knew I would make it as soon as I got a break. We made it, we've got our own business and I've always loved her for it. I think the big secret of our marriage is the decision that we made years ago to at least be good friends. We decided that we'd treat each other as well as we did our friends. You know how you're always happy and put your best face on with friends. It seems to me that if you can't be as nice to each other as you are to your friends, something's wrong."

I'd never thought of it quite like that, have you! It's beautiful really and it has obviously worked for them.

If a long happy marriage is so helpful to so many people, what's the reason? It seems obvious. As Carolyn has told me for years, "Someone has to think you're the most special person in the whole world, or you just can't make it." I don't know whether she's handing me orders or just saying how it is with her, but she's right.

A 91-year-old man in a nursing home once said it like this: "The young people think we are unreasonably demanding. They feel all our needs are met. We are comfortably clothed, housed, well fed, protected from hazards, provided with companionship and diversion. Our greatest need is not met. It is one we *never* outgrow. It is the need to feel CHERISHED BY SOMEONE — to know there is a place we belong."

Is divorce the end of the line, is the world over? No, but it's a sign two students flunked their violin lessons. Is it possible to remarry and find happiness? Sure, it's just that we have to be careful. We've got two musical dropouts starting a new band. That's why so many second and third marriages are worse than the first.

If we learn from our mistakes and then apply it, we can do wonders. I think divorce is a horrendous insult to two people. I don't care who's at fault or what the cause. It's an insult and a "major life upheaval." I think the only worse insult is to not get divorced and let "hostility become a habit." You can't just dismiss two, five, ten or twenty years of life with someone by obtaining a legal document. It's been an emotional commitment and it cannot be undone with a legal scrap of paper.

One of my patients is 50-years-old and an "upper" to have come in. She's on marriage number four and it's great. (Much to my surprise.) She's learned a lot, not just experienced a lot, and after caring for her I'm sure she tried within her ability with the first three marriages. You can just tell it. She told me before her current marriage, "I'm determined to risk it again. I want a partner, and I will be myself this time. I want someone who can live without alcohol, who has tolerance beyond himself and I'll have to 'see love — not hear it.'" She was clever. She made him lunch and at noon would take it out to the plant where he worked the year they were going together.

She said, "I was interested in seeing how he interacted with his fellow employees." She married a rare jewel that anyone would be happy with, and after several years they're a joy to see. He sees the beauty in her and she in him. It can happen and does, but you have to take some personal inventory.

Someone has said, "Divorce is the result of two neurotics not working out their problems." I prefer just two "people" not working on their problems. I have often felt that if we all spent one-tenth the effort making a marriage work, that we do building a good case for divorce, we would all have eternal marital bliss.

I agree with the marriage experts on all four points discussed a few paragraphs back. The woman changing status has been a large factor. The Womens' Liberation Movement has been necessary and helpful in one area. Equal pay for equal work and equal opportunity to work. Beyond that, I don't see much. As one nurse, high in the organizational level and a dedicated Liberation Movement worker, told me: "I'm beginning to have second thoughts about the whole movement. There's a lot of stress attached to some of our new positions that I don't think most of us really want. I've got headaches now like I never had and I don't think it's worth it." I think the Liberation Movement is one of the saddest offshoots of our marital problems. It's a logical offshoot at first glance, and if I'd lost at love I'd be looking for a flock of similar birds. Now, hold it all of you happily married "libbers." I didn't say lost at love with a *man*. I just say lost at love! We can lose at love all by ourselves and from where I sit, that's the way I see it.

The newspaper recently carried an "Alice Does Day" article. The day was set aside for women to quit work for the day to show support for women to protest a system that "ignores, oppresses, rapes, brutalizes, imprisons, confines, and restricts" Alice in her potential. Does our system really do all that? If I ever begin to suspect that my wife and two daughters are oppressed, ignored, raped, brutalized, imprisoned, confined and restricted I will be leading the march in their behalf.

If I'm going to lead a march, I want all the marchers behind me on my side. Carrying a protest banner is awfully hard work if the message isn't clear. I'm not saying the "libbers" haven't convinced me. My concern is that they haven't convinced themselves.

A case in point. One of the lady lawyers who has worked on the national scene was in town and interviewed by a reporter-person (male, I assume, but the paper didn't say which). She explained the term "lawyer" is neuter and has nothing to do with sex. So far I'm convinced. Her boss is to face her as an attorney-person.

Interestingly enough, she is a very attractive "blondperson" and she had a two-column closeup full-length picture of her in the paper, sitting with her hemline carefully draped high above her knee. When the reporter told her she was "sexy" she said, "Oh, I've never been called 'sexy' before! Are you going to print that? It's a lifetime dream."

Probably the first reported case of a sexy, neuter attorney. But she must be sincere. Any "person" who is so attractive, has her hair done so meticulously, who wears such a stunning outfit and whose makeup is flawless — all for other "women-persons" — just *has* to be sincere.

My nurse, Dorothy, teases me (I think). She says, "I know it's a tough world being a man. You have to shave everyday."

The world will never be a tough place for men, as long as they can share it with women — not "persons." I just don't want us having separate camps.

It's the same with the "swingers." I read a book recently detailing the thrills of swingers. It began by defining swingers by Webster's dictionary. The dictionary they used defined swinging as a "pendulum motion, a back and forth rhythm" and the author found that this was rather suggestive in itself.

I guess it's which edition of Websters you use. Mine says, swinging:

1. to move rapidly in an arc (to me that means moving in an incomplete circle)
2. to sway or cause to sway back and forth (to me this is indecision)
3. to hang so as to move freely back and forth in a curve (this can cause dizziness)
4. to be executed by hanging (we're getting closer)

To me "to swing" is to dangle. And this is what you do when you're at the bitter end of your mental rope.

The book then lists the names and addresses of numerous "swingers clubs" all across the country. That seems odd. To let everyone in on all the fun. When I catch fish, few people know where I did it.

I see many housewives suddenly deciding the magazine articles are right. "Is Marriage Wrecking Your Career?" How can it? If you're married and you have children, marriage *is* your career! The career better come later, or sooner if you want one. It is tempting to heed the call for personal liberation the day the two small children have diarrhea and the third is sent home from school for misbehavior. It doesn't help if "hubby" is passed over for a promotion the same day and the septic tank plugged up, but if you can hang in there the rewards are terrific. The job at the bank sounds a lot more glamorous and exciting and you'll no doubt find plenty of sympathizers with your plot, but it doesn't work. If you've got children, *you're* going to have to spend time with them, it's just a matter of when. You can spend it with them while they're young and growing up and enjoy them the rest of your lives, or you can postpone spending time with them for the first 16 years and then begin to spend it in the juvenile courts and have headaches the rest of your life. It seems a little confusing. We're talking about raising a generation of "love starved" children yet the heat is on for more "daycare centers" to rectify our problem. The more daycare centers we build, the more we will have to convert later on into juvenile detention centers! Those first few years from 3 to 6 are just too formative in the child's life. You either get it going for you then or you never do. Some mothers have been put to the test — they've had no choice but to get out and make a living for themselves and their children, and I've seen some do some super-human jobs. They spend all the time they can with their children and the children know it. This is a little different than the majority I see where the mother spends all the time away that she can, and the children know it. That's when physicans begin to see the children coming in with symptoms and the panel lights flashing. That's when we begin to see the stomach aches, the nervous excess energy, and the rebellion and poor grades at school. I've known quite a few wives, with devoted husbands who've decided that having two or three children and rapidly approaching the age of 30 or 35 was too much and they complained of being "unfulfilled." I get the funny feeling that they've "read it, before they've felt it." I'm not picking on the gals. Without three special gals in my world, I wouldn't make it. I can't afford the luxury of being "down" on women.

It's time that we dropped the "just a housewife" putdown that I keep hearing. I know of no career that is more demanding or as rewarding as being a housewife. To guide a few children from infancy to the happy, well-adjusted adult requires talent and understanding that can't be handled by "just" anyone. If you doubt me, look around you.

The skirt-chasing husband very often helps the undecided gal come to a decision and I don't blame her for looking for help. All I'm saying is that we ought to be looking for help in the right direction when we need it, from our friends, our children, and within and not by joining what has been called a group of "oppressed, ignored, raped, brutalized, imprisoned, confined and restricted members." I'm sure we'll no doubt have a "men's movement" if we don't already, and it will sing the same song with just a lower pitch.

Henri F. Amiel said: "It is dangerous to abandon oneself to the luxury of grief; it deprives one of courage and even the wish of recovery."

Limping along with either a men's or a women's liberation movement may reinforce your feelings of grief, but it does little to remove such feelings. I'm all for liberation for anyone who doesn't have it, but getting liberated is a personal responsibility. No committee can do it for you.

Marriage should be too much fun to have it and its side effects become the source of most of our and our children's physical and emotional ills. We've got to review why we are staying married, what our older and wiser friends are saying about marriage. We have to realize that being "special" to someone is all important. We've got to replace our fears and distrust with warmth in action as well as words. We've got to look within ourselves. We've got to reconsider the old proverb, "Sticks and stones may break my bones, but words will never hurt me." That's not what I see. I'd change it to, "Sticks and stones *only* break my bones but words are sure to kill me." Words are powerful, and tend to echo a long time after they are spoken or written. As one 16-year-old boy told me about his alcoholic father: "He only beat me once, and I wish he would more often instead of killing me with words."

We've got to get some different books on the coffee table. Then we won't have to be concerned like one mother who came in wondering about her daughter's Sunday School paper on which she had written the Ten Commandments for a little quiz. She had them all perfect except, "thou shalt not admit adultery." We nervously agreed that it was no doubt a spelling error and not a sign of the times. We can't have all the books lying around with all the answers in them before the children even know the questions.

How about living together so that man-made marriage certificate doesn't wreck a "meaningful relationship?" Let's look at one.

"The tension is terrible. I'm divorced now, and have been living with someone else for three months. It was okay for a while. I now feel very wrong about it. My folks don't agree with me. I'm so tired of it all. I'm Ms. so and so at work, Mrs. so and so at other times. I was married 14 years and it didn't work out. I didn't want this one not to work out, too. We've tried it three months and now I scream at the slightest things — even my children. This is pure hell. This is worse than marriage. I feel that if I do the slightest thing wrong, he'll walk out and I guess I can't blame him. That's our deal. The kids want to know how soon they're going to

96

get their new name. God, I didn't think they'd care and my daughter is sick all the time with one thing after another."

Some of these thoughts can be the building materials used to rebuild a marriage, but they're just the "raw materials" for us to build with. Merely reading them won't do it. We've got to use them and start rebuilding now. We can't wait to use them on our "second honeymoon" once every two or three years. It's our marriage and our health.

Plastic surgery won't give a marriage a new face, even though it is often tried. If plastic surgery will help you feel better, fine, but don't do it to "solve a problem." Plastic surgery isn't done between the ears. If a marriage is based merely on anatomical perfection, it is a poor investment and will get worse as time goes on.

One fellow, age 24, with two marriages already behind him admitted his 23-year-old fiance for "plastic breast surgery." He came running down the hall and knocked furiously on the surgeon's dressing room door.

"I have to see Dr. Ralls right away," he said.

Dr. Ralls was dressing for surgery, walked over and they chatted outside his door.

The doctor came back fuming, "I don't know who the nut is, him or his fiance, now he has decided he wants her fanny changed, too."

This guy's been around. He is taking no chances on marriage number three. The poor girl is only 23 and isn't even married yet. If she needs a major overhaul now, someone's going to have a maintenance bill he won't believe after the first annual inspection.

Samuel Johnson said, "To be happy at home is the ultimate benefit of all ambition." He might have said, to be happy at home is the ultimate in health.

I'm totally convinced our number one health hazard is to be unhappy at home.

7 – Is It My Job Or Am I Picking Leaves From The Trees?

Upon every face is written the record of the life man has led; the prayers, the aspirations, the disappointments, all he hoped to be and was not, all are written there; nothing is hidden nor indeed can be.

Elbert Hubbard

Next to marriage and all of its related issues, our occupations come in second as a health hazard. I'm not talking about jobs with known health threats. I'm more concerned with the everyday jobs we all pursue, whether at the office or factory or in the home. It may be the type of work, a new boss or new position, or fellow personnel that get the blame.

Before putting marriage to rest, it should be pointed out that the road to health problems caused by our jobs frequently take a detour through the marriage, so that at first the job affects the marriage and this in turn affects the health of one or both partners. It always amazes me how much the wife is affected by her husband being unhappy with his work. I think that many times it affects her more because long after the husband has cursed and stormed about it, and forgotten it, the wife is still upset about sending him off to provide for the family at a job he detests (or thinks he does).

Work has been variously defined as a "neurosis," our reason for being, and something to be avoided at all costs. Mark Twain said that work made him nervous even when someone else was doing it. The truth, as usual, is probably somewhere down the middle. With so many different definitions, work must be interpreted in different lights by different individuals. I think this is an important point and have asked many times, "Is it your job or your interpretation of your job?" There is a big difference here and it's frequently more a matter of perspective than the job itself. Someone has said that people are like plants and need to be re-potted now and then. (Ben Syra said, "Gnaw the bone which has fallen to thy lot.") Each statement carries its own truth. I think it is much better to "re-pot" ourselves than to continue gnawing the bone if we have lost our teeth and the bone is in splinters.

One accepted authority on stress has alluded to the fact that certain occupations are without reward and people in these jobs must certainly look elsewhere for their daily means. I couldn't disagree more and his lack of contact with people or "patients" is showing. He singles out garbage men as one group that is relatively hopeless in this world. My home "garbage collector" greets me once a week with more gusto and a bigger smile than I ever see in the doctor's room or at the hospital. After 15 years I've yet to hear a disgruntled comment from him and he seems to be happy to be starting another day. For some reason I have my share of people in garbage work and I see no reason in asking what attracts them to me, but one things stands out: I see very little of them except for routine driving examinations or annual physicals and I never hear the husband, wife or children complain of their role in this world. The people in garbage and sanitary work that I take care of are often in the office only for "shots" for their next overseas vacation. I'm sure there are miserable garbage collectors in this world, but I strongly suspect the miserable doctors far outnumber them. Again, it's a matter of interpretation in the beholder's eyes. Let's look at an example:

Murray is 48 and came in with symptoms of an ulcer. I examined him and ordered the proverbial "Upper GI." We were in luck; Murray had an ulcer and he and I reviewed the film with much excitement. "There it is. Sure, I can see it; no doubt about it. Well, that explains why I've been hurting then. I knew I had one. It's that blasted job of mine," he said.

"What do you do?" I asked.

"Oh, I work in the appliance department of a department store."

"Pretty hectic is it?" I asked.

"Yeah, you can say that again, I've never seen so many unhappy, complaining people in my life. No one smiles, they're all so grouchy. I can just feel my stomach go into knots. I can't take it much longer, I know that," he moaned.

I treated Murray with the usual diets and medications and we made progress in a snail-like manner. He continued to have pain and continued to complain that it was his job and he felt it was ridiculous to expect him to improve as long as he kept his same job.

On one of the later visits, I zeroed in on the job a little more.

"Just what do you do with appliances, Murray?" I asked, "repair them or something?"

"In a sense," he replied. "I get them if they're not working."

"Then you pick up appliances and repair them?" I groped.

"No, not exactly," he said. "They just bring them to my window if they're unhappy."

"Your window?" I asked, "What is your window?"

"It's the Customer Satisfaction window," he offered dejectedly.

"Customer Satisfaction window?" It didn't sound right. "If they were satisfied, you wouldn't have a window would you

Murray?" I asked. "Wouldn't it be better called the Customer Dissatisfaction window or Complaint Department?"

Murray grinned, "I suppose so. I just never thought of it like that," he said.

"And you wonder why everyone is unhappy and grouchy?" I asked. "What are they supposed to say when they bring in that $30 toaster they've had for six days that doesn't do as good a job as the 18-year-old one they pitched out? You really ought to go out each morning and interpret the sign to say, 'Complaint Department' and expect everyone to be loaded with complaints. It's your job. But you aren't the one who made the toaster. You really aren't guilty. You can show concern and begin to remedy the situation with a replacement or whatever, but *you* didn't do it. You aren't the cause. You're part of the solution and that helps."

Murray sat back with a distant look. "I'll try it. I guess I've been crazy for 20 years to expect anything but complaints. I think that will help a lot and I don't know why I haven't thought of it like that before."

Murray changed his approach, his "Upper GI" x-ray and his health and outlook in general. He had trouble at first, but he just kept repeating, "I expect it." This approach could have saved Murray considerable trouble twenty years ago, but power to him that he can see it now. It wasn't his job that caused his ulcer. The ulcer healed nicely while on "the job." It was Murray's *interpretation* of the job. The final ironic twist is that one and one-half years after retiring, Murray is back in with stomach complaints again and says, "It's my job. If only I could get it back. I've got to be busy. This retirement business is no good!"

The contrast one morning between two patients in adjoining rooms was too much. In one room was a 38-year-old woman who wanted a note for Social Security stating that she was "disabled." After I had examined her completely, I asked her "on what condition do you base your disability?"

Without a blink she replied, "Because all work makes me nervous. I've tried a variety of jobs but it's always the same."

I explained that it made me equally nervous to fill out disability forms for healthy people knowing full well that I was footing the bill and would recommend that she work on the problem, not on retirement. She left mortally wounded that of all people a "doctor" wouldn't put her on easy street. I next received a letter from the California Welfare Department wanting her past medical history so they could expedite her "benefits."

In the next room was a 79-year-old man who was in with a sore back. He had slipped at work digging up four to eight-year-old trees in a nursery. He has had diabetes, hypertension and mild heart failure for years. When still a child a wagon rolled over him and broke his hip, so his left leg is two inches shorter than the right. He hobbles with a hopeless shuffle and how he digs trees and lifts them out with a 70 to 130 pound ball of dirt I really don't know. But he does and he loves it. He complains about his job in an entirely different way. He is worried that the nursery may be closed down in a year or two because a freeway access may need the land. I was tempted to put them in a room and let them share ideas, but my better judgment prevailed.

The contrast, however, was so great. Here was a 38-year-old wanting to stop work, because it made her "nervous" and a 78-year-old who was nervous because his work was stopping.

Well, this all sounds simple enough. All we have to do is take any job and "interpret" it right and we'll be happy. Or is it so simple? Some of us are unable to interpret our jobs differently, at least at this moment in our life, and a change or "re-potting" can often be a fresh start. If it is us and our interpretation of the job, the next one may be worse. Even if the next job is worse, the world won't end.

The change can well be worth it if it does nothing more than lead us to the obvious conclusion. We will have to change some thoughts as well as our job.

One of the most grievous errors a wife can make, in my opinion, is to discourage a husband from changing jobs or even considering it. I can think of so many cases in which the husband has "peaked out" in his chosen field and feels in desperate need of a change, but is thwarted by his wife at the very mention of it. She has good reason. She knows what "living" costs. She probably pays the bills. She is fully aware that you can't live on dreams, and insecurity usually rears its head. It's "safer" to stay at the same old grind with its monthly check than to gamble on her husband's ability to paint watercolors for a living. She is no doubt aware that Michaelangelo and Rembrandt both died paupers. She reaches the logical but disastrous conclusion. She stomps her feet and the dreams are cooled, but they smoulder forever.

The husband also reaches a logical conclusion. He is to continue a second 20 years of endeavor he has long since mentally abandoned. I have never seen it work. He doesn't mention it again, but the storm clouds slowly gather behind the usual "calm." He will turn to something and it won't be watercolors. The marriage invariably suffers.

It's a hard decision, I know, but I am convinced it is much better to try "the dream." It is really the safest route. The wife can't lose by giving her full support. If the dream is a success, as it usually is, because of the husband's newly found energy, all ends well. If not, two people may become closer for it. The old job may well be waiting or a new one can be found. It is much better to wreck the savings account than the marriage.

Some jobs can have only one interpretation. Raymond, age

34, has such a job. Raymond came in with so many symptoms and diagnoses that to list them would finish the chapter. His job had resulted in numerous transfers across the country. Numerous physicians had seen him and each of his symptoms had been assigned an accommodating diagnosis. I filled 38 lines on his chart with his symptoms and past diagnoses. I knew that few could be real or he couldn't have walked in. It took two appointments to "hear" his problems. On the third appointment I was able to examine him completely and no organic problem was found.

Raymond worked for a large international corporation with numerous retail outlets. His job was to find prospective buyers for the problem stores. These were the stores that had been continual losers since the opening day and had resulted in one failure after another.

Raymond began in a voice that said it all. "I am probably the most unhappy person that you have ever met. I have been for four years. I think I need a shrink; my wife is sure of it. We are in the throes of a separation at this point which neither of us wants, for ourselves or our five children. My wife is rebelling against my rebellion. I hate my job. I have been at it for ten years. I'm tired of screwing people and that's my job, screwing people. Pressure and subterfuge, that's what I do. I literally 'ruin' people. We have what we call the 'warm body principle.' "

"Warm body principle?" I asked. "What's that?"

"You know," he continued, "you've got a store that will never make a cent, it never has, it never will, it's in the wrong spot. You get a guy in and you know what's going to happen. He'll go broke; he'll have a divorce; he'll file bankruptcy and his credit will be ruined. I've done this fifty times in the last three years. It bothers me. I get extremely close to these guys and their families, they're really nice people."

Should Raymond interpret the job differently? I think he has interpreted it right. It's sad that the job even exists. It no longer does for Raymond. As soon as he notified the boss that he was quitting, nearly all of his symptoms began to disappear. Raymond didn't need a "shrink." He was interpreting things right. If he had kept on, he would have lost a battle with the personal social or civil war that we all fight and he would have required treatment for an emotional or mental illness which he didn't have. I would have been more concerned about his mental health if all this had agreed with him. This is all too often what happens. We get treated for an emotional problem or mental disease, because we're seeing the social and civil war the way it is.

A large number of in depth studies have been done to try and correlate certain types of work to certain health problems. Several studies have been done correlating high-stress executive jobs to heart disease and ulcers. The findings are somewhat convincing and this is not too surprising. I have to question the interpretation of the studies though. Certainly the head of a large company is going to have a lot of important daily decisions to make and that's stress in the raw. But let's back up. Did the manager just suddenly fall into a position of high stress or has he been expending a terrific amount of stress the past 20 or 30 years trying to land the top job with the most stress of all? There's a difference. That's why the study showing a relationship of coronary artery disease to high-pressure white collar jobs needs another look.

I'm convinced that if you took a top executive and placed him in a blue collar and gave him a street sweeping job in San Francisco, he would generate all kinds of stress. For one thing, he wouldn't know what to do with all the extra money he would be earning. He would worry about missing a piece of paper or a shred of litter. He would be worried about beating the other street sweeper on the other side of the street to the end of the block. He would try to be the one with the most loads of litter at the end of the day. He would probably have a coronary trying to get his push cart across the intersection before the amber light turned red.

Does the nature of the job create the stress or does the stress dictate the nature of the job?

I have one patient in his late 40s who owns a large string of successful stores, any one of which would wrap him and his wife in total security. He is continually grasping to add another store to his chain. He came into my office with moderately severe chest pain one day.

"What's the cause, Doc?" he said, pacing the room. "It hit me last night and I've had a little bit of it off and on for a month."

He continued to pace back and forth across the examining room glancing at his digital watch.

"Bill, sit down. Let's talk about this and then I'll get you in a gown and we'll examine you. We'll need an electrocardiogram for one thing." He continued pacing the floor despite three distinct pleas by me for him to sit down.

"Well, I don't have time for all that," he fumed. "Can't you just give me something for the chest pain?"

"Sure, I can pick something out of my hat, but I really don't know what the problem is, much less how to treat it," I said.

"Well, how long would a cardiogram take anyway?" he grudgingly asked.

"About 15 or 20 minutes," I said.

"That long, huh? Well, I'll tell you what — I've got a meeting, if it gets worse I'll call you," he hollered as he strolled out the door.

Bill has three children and a delightful wife. I've been in their dream home — it's elegant. I've admitted Bill's wife three times for "nervous breakdowns." Before I admitted her the last time I sat beside her bed in their palatial home and heard a sorry tale of woe.

"Doctor, what's wrong with me anyway?" she asked. "I can't make a simple decision anymore. I can't even decide what to wear without changing clothes ten times. I spend all my time holding back a flood of tears. I had dinner out with Bill two weeks ago and have hardly seen him since. He took me and 'his books' to dinner. When the waiter came to take our orders I ordered and the waiter turned to Bill and waited patiently. Bill didn't even know he was there. I nudged him and he looked up."

"Oh, hi there, I'll have the same as her," he fired and went back to his books.

"I had a drink after dinner, and just sat watching him plan his next business triumph," she continued. "I guess I have everything and yet I don't have a damned thing. You probably don't understand."

I understood completely. She had everything this world has for sale and nothing this world has to give. She is missing one vital ingredient that we talked about earlier: someone to think she is the most special person in the world.

She spent another two weeks in the hospital recovering from her nervous breakdown. Is she suffering from mental disease or is she reading the crystal ball clearly? Does *she* need treatment or does the situation she is in need the treatment?

High-stress job or high-stress man? How many businesses will he need to acquire before he can find peace of mind and relax? I wouldn't guess and I'm sure he hasn't even considered it. I've lost track of this couple now. Bill called back and was furious because I wouldn't treat his chest pain over the phone. He literally doesn't have time to have the proper coronary attack, but I'm sure he'll make time. The tragic and frustrating part is that once a person sets his sail on this track it requires a capsizing of the ship to make him ever consider changing course. I have found that precious few are open to suggestion before disaster strikes.

I had another lady, age 50, in the hospital with "total exhaustion." Her husband was a rapidly climbing executive with a major clothing manufacturing firm. She was on the phone everytime I went into another room. It sounded as if she was planning a large party of some kind. I finally asked what all the plans were about.

"We're giving a party for 40 couples tomorrow night at our house," she stated.

"That's impossible, " I stammered. "You're not ready to go home yet. You're going to still be here."

"I know," she reassured me, "but that doesn't matter. Edward (her husband) is going to be there. He has to be. It's our turn, you know, and it's expected of us if Ed is going to keep climbing. I'm just trying to help with the details."

Edward had called me and explained that he had wanted her "fixed up for good" this time. He was tired of these emotional "flare ups." That seemed simple enough. Do all the usual tests and have all the usual consultants look in, check out each system thoroughly. Discharge her on four different pills: two "uppers" and two "downers" and make sure it doesn't happen again. Edward didn't quite make it to the hospital during the ten days she was in, but he "called every day he got a chance."

Here was a lady "entertaining" 80 people from her hospital bed. Now that's homespun warmth and hospitality. It's just possible we've lost something when the hostess can't make it to "her" party anymore. And not only that but she's trying to recover from an "emotional flare-up" and push her husband up the corporate ladder at the same time.

This is what I call losing sight of ground zero. Of getting back to a few simple basic things. It's hard to do, but we have to do it. How? We each have to find our own approach.

Sometimes I have to drive to a hallowed little acreage in the country to get back to ground zero. I find getting out in the trees, digging in the garden or orchard, running an old tractor or just sitting on a stump helps me to take stock of myself. What do I want or need from life? What am I willing to offer for my needs? What are the true pleasures in this world and how many thousands do they cost, or are they relatively low priced and abundant? Will I ever have the time I need to cover half of the things I want to get to? Am I going too fast or too slow? Am I sacrificing any small part of my mental or physical make up for something that isn't worth it, or is anything worth such a sacrifice? How many things am I doing for profit? And how many things am I doing for fun? Have I sold out to the highest available salary?

Are Carolyn and I seeing enough of each other? Do I wish she would have come out today with me or do I need the day alone? Maybe it's best; I'll enjoy her more after we've had a mutual break or is that being selfish? Do we have enough time left in this short life to spend many days apart? Are Pam and Sue, our daughters, getting prepared for a life full of love; not fantastic achievements, but a life of love? I came to grips with this long ago when they quit their piano lessons. How could they do it to "us." I know the teacher is quitting, but there are hundreds more; we bought a piano and invested time and money. They're doing so well and Carolyn and I have nervously basked in three perfect annual recitals.

It's just not right, or is it? Or, have I tried to set up a franchise and failed? I'll buy the piano and pay for the lessons and Carolyn will drive for months and years, that's the good news. The bad news (and not so clearly stated) is that two gals had better practice and play better each month and not talk to boys or the deal is off. The trouble is that *we* set the "deal" up and they had little choice but to go along with it. I had to find ground zero. Would sitting in front of this ivory-laced musical wonder really bring them happiness? Could we really be guaranteed they wouldn't notice boys sooner or later anyway? (And would I really want that?)

They quit. Sue misses it like an alarm clock and Pam sneaks in a few bars when I'm gone (I understand). That's fine with me, but I had to have a talk with myself.

Carolyn and I had a good deal going. Someday we just might have seen one or both names on the concert program. I could have used that because my one and only piano lesson ended halfway through with me in tears and my disinterested teacher with a handful of remnants from a three-cornered ruler.

Is anyone squirming a bit? Maybe you don't have to. Perhaps you're smarter and aren't trying to see the world through your children's conquests. I hope so. They won't let you pull it off anyway and I am totally convinced that neither music lessons or athletic activities will postpone puberty indefinitely for a child or parent.

One family in my practice would not attend their son's wedding because he was headed for stardom in football. Mother and dad had severed all ties, because they feared that marriage in college would wreck his career or, more bluntly, their careers. They didn't say this of course; the girl was not of the right mold, they were too young and they didn't have the money. They have a great marriage, early fame and have money, but the folks aren't bending a bit even though the children have tried making amends. Someone stole their share of the spoils and they don't like it! The parents have lost their ground zero. Their "value-scope" needs adjustment.

Each one of us has to find our own way of regaining perspective. We need all the aids, books and gimmicks we can find. Carolyn and I get a new lease on life at our small acreage. It completely recharges us. I feel we have to recharge somehow. Our batteries are on discharge all day at work, we have to have an equal time on "recharge" or we deplete the battery. For every hour on discharge we need an hour on recharge. If you can get it each night on the couch being hypnotized with television, great, but it won't do it for most of my patients and I doubt that it will do it for you and me. It's not that "recharging." I saw a recent television survey that showed that 30 percent of the television audience will not change stations between 8 p.m. and 11 p.m. no matter what is being shown. That's not recharging, that's emotional babysitting!

You can't recharge by running faster or working harder to keep from looking in your "value-scope." We can compare life to a candle. You only have so much wax available. If you light a few extra wicks, you can get a brighter glow, but it won't last as long. It's the same with your body; if you want to drive it relentlessly, you can for awhile, but keep up your life insurance so your spouse and new mate can live in style.

Some of us can put stress in any job even if we have to go looking for it.

One dear little 80-year-old woman nearly lost her life by turning her gardening and yardwork into a stressful situation. She took great pride in keeping a perfect yard. That was her fulltime job and she drove herself into impossible extremes. A neighbor found her under a tree screaming with pain. He called an ambulance and she was brought into my office. She was on the stretcher and in severe pain with an obvious broken hip. I asked her what happened.

"I fell from the top of the tree while picking the leaves," she moaned.

"Picking the what?" I asked.

"Picking the leaves," she returned. "I like to get them before they fall and make a mess in the yard!"

She was serious. The neighbor confirmed it. She had always picked the leaves from the trees before they had a chance to fall.

How many of us "pick the leaves from the trees?" I see it so often. It's like trying to sail dead into the wind or swimming upstream. It's hard work and we don't make much progress. We're going to take charge; we can do it; we're all powerful. It's too much for most people, but *I* can do it. I know I shouldn't work three jobs, but someday when the extra car and new television are paid for, I'll relax. The wife plans to stop work after the kids are through all of their orthodontia. The kids would be better off with teeth like walrus' tusks and having mother home when they get off the school bus so they can say "nothing" when she asks, "What did you do in school today?"

We're all so busy picking the leaves from the trees we've forgotten how beautiful it is to watch them fall. We're rushing it. We're not going to let nature take its course. We'll help it, we'll speed it up, we'll do it our way and a lot faster. We're going to swim upstream and we're going to pay a high price for it. That's stress in all its glory and the reward is a health problem sooner or later. It's like a sign I once saw that said, "God — give me patience. Hurry!"

A 38-year-old man came in with chest pains which proved to be angina. He was working two long jobs. I advised him to quit one of the jobs immediately.

He said, "I can't right now, doctor, I've got my eye on a new red pickup. After I get it, I'll quit one job if you really think I should."

Neither I nor his wife could convince him to quit. He died of a coronary before he ever got his new red pickup.

What about the children's jobs? What about the "job" of going to school? Stress is where you find it or make it.

Tim, a second grade boy, was brought in by his mother for a check-up to see if he had a medical problem that would account for his slow learning. He had flunked first grade and had repeated it. Now he was in the process of flunking second grade. He checked out fine and was as smart as the rest, I was sure.

"What's the problem, Tim?" I asked.

"I don't know," he said sadly. "I flunked last year in Tacoma. We moved to Portland this year and I'm flunking again, I guess."

"Is school hard for you?" I asked.

"No, at least I don't think so. I guess I'm just a born loser," he said. This chilled me. Here was a boy with an adult vocabulary and a lot of insight and already felt like a born loser in the second grade. I see lots of children like this who become frustrated and "hyperactive." We than start to medicate and set up special courses and counseling and the long familiar story unfolds. These kids are not short on intelligence. They're not born losers; they're man-made losers and you and I get the credit. They're leaving home with the "learning switch" turned to off; they're not "available" for learning. We have 92 names for the hyperactive child syndrome, which should tell us something.

We can't blame the teacher or the school system. The teacher may be the most gifted teacher in the country, but he or she is on the receiving end. If Tim comes to school with the learning switch in the "off" position, the most we could expect is failure, rebellion and hyperactivity. No child can sit there and "take it." No drugs, sugar-free diets or counseling will bail us out. It just doesn't work. They may help, but they're only temporary patches.

What causes the switch to be thrown to off? It's not the school "job" nor the child's interpretation of it. Problems in the home, whether out in the open or partially camouflaged, are the usual cause. It may be a problem that only the child sees such as mother being gone all day. It may be friction between the parents that is poorly concealed. The children see it long before we're talking about it. We underestimate our children's perception. They have us "pegged" long before we do them. They can't stand insecurity any more at their early ages than you and I can later on and I'm talking about love not financial security. Kids don't remember the year dad cleaned up financially or mother was chairman of the civic club, but they do remember the mountains, the campsite at the beach, the afternoon at the park and the tower of books that you've read together.

Somehow we've developed the idea that raising our children

is someone else's job. It doesn't work. It's our job anyway we interpret it.

One mother brought her teenage daughter in for an examination. During the exam the mother proudly said, "Sally, tell doctor where we're going next."

"Oh, mother, he doesn't care," Sally squirmed.

"Yes he does, tell him," mother urged.

Sally was too embarrassed.

"Well, I'll tell him," mother snorted. "We're going to give a note to the school principal. He sent home a note saying Sally wasn't doing well in math and wants to talk to me."

"That sounds like a start. You can be glad he's concerned," I replied.

"Well, I'm not talking to him," she said. "Sally's going to give him a note from me while I wait in the car, aren't you, Sally? Show the note to Dr. Fisher."

Sally handed me the note with a shy thrust.

It read, "Dear Sir, If Sally is having trouble with her math, you have my permission to teach it to her."

Where is Sally's learning switch thrown to? Where is it likely to stay? Is it Sally's job or her and mother's interpretation of it?

Look at your job. Should you continue to "gnaw" the bone or do you need re-potting? Only you can decide. Is it the job that's causing symptoms or are you trying to pick the leaves before they fall?

One patient of mine is a longshoreman and has suffered a hearing loss from working in the holds of ships. We talked about it and I told him I felt it was unfortunate that we had not been more "noise conscious" in the past.

He looked up and said, "Oh, I don't mind at all, that's a small price to pay for all it's done for me. It's fed and clothed us all and educated all my children."

If our jobs, whatever they are, are causing a good share of our health problems then retirement should be the cure. Let's take a look.

8 – The Last For Which The First Was Made

Victor Frankhl said, "We who lived in concentration camps can remember the men who walked through the huts comforting others, giving away their last piece of bread. They may have been few in number, but they offer sufficient proof that everything can be taken from a man but one thing: the last of the human freedoms to choose one's attitude in any given set of circumstances, to choose one's own way."

What attitudes are we going to have in retirement? Most likely, the very same attitudes we carried with us through our working years. We can put more stress in our "retirement job" than we ever did in our active job. Those of us who picked the leaves from the trees during our active working years usually start chopping the limbs from the trees in retirement. We can't turn off the habits and attitudes of the past 30 years the day that we retire. For a good many people retirement is when the trouble really starts and the Association of Retired People can't cure it. That job we've been blaming for the past 30 years may actually have been keeping body and soul together, even though it took its toll.

I usually begin to see the wife with a variety of symptoms one to two years before her husband retires. The very thought of retirement upsets the wife and she comes in with headaches and fatigue or "GI" problems.

"It's just an effort to get up each morning," she tells me. The husband retires and he does just that. He gets rid of all his tools and his hobby equipment and they move into a retirement center with a 10 x 10 foot yard and a garage so sterile that you could set up a smorgasbord on the floor.

"I don't have to do nothing now," I frequently hear. "I've retired. I've worked all my life. I've worked enough. I got rid of all my tools. I'm just going to take life easy and have fun."

Have fun! The wife doesn't see it that way. Shortly after he retires the husband begins to come in with symptoms. He's beginning to notice his wife's resentment and he doesn't like it and doesn't understand it. It isn't the "grand vacation" that he had planned. The highlight of any vacation is returning and telling the gang "how great it was." We can't do this with the retirement vacation, it never ends.

One elderly lady told me, "My husband and I had had a wonderful marriage for 40 years. He had been retired for five years before he died and the last five years had been hard for both of us. It embarrasses me to even talk about it. We weren't prepared at all, either of us, we couldn't take 24 hours a day of each other. I think it upset me more than it did him. He didn't get out with the fellows at all and I didn't want to hurt him by leaving him alone. He's been gone four years and I'm ashamed to say but I'm just beginning to relax and be myself again. I've quit shaking and my headaches are gone. That's terrible to say isn't it, doctor?"

It's only terrible because it's true. What happened to our "grow old with me, the best is yet to come" bit? That's the way it should be and can be.

One lady recently told me, "You'd appreciate a good man like I've got. We tease a lot, we talk a lot, we discuss things. We are so busy and have so much to do with our separate and mutual interests. He's been retired three years and we have all the extra time that we've never had before. We've been trying to make up for lost time. We enjoy ourselves, so of course we enjoy each other."

The attraction of the retirement center seems ever more popular. In my experience it's the first big mistake for a lot of people. The first hazard is moving away from your life-long friends and neighbors to a "secure easy living" center.

One husband called me out to the retirement center to see his wife for a "heart condition." When I got there his wife was sitting in a chair, ashen in color with her pulse racing. He was covered with scratches and dried blood on his face. They had obviously had a good fight. Why? The husband had said the drapery men were coming at 11 a.m. and his wife had argued they were coming at noon, and the fight was on. That was it, the main worry for the day. He had been in active business management before retirement and she had been occupied with her numerous clubs and large garden. They had moved away from their large home, their large circle of friends, their clubs and business organizations. They now had each day to "enjoy" each other.

I've had other patients come in depressed and upset after their monthly "fun trip" to the beach. The fun trip turns out to be a disaster. One lady came in wanting "anti-depressants" after the monthly fun outing. She sat by the same people on the bus coming and going to the beach and heard the same complaints both ways. When they arrived at the restaurant at the beach, one busload had to wait as the restaurant could not accommodate all of them at once. By the time the first load comes out berating the food, the restaurant doesn't have a chance, and neither does the next busload.

Another lady said, "Our home really swings. The biggest excitement of the day is trying to guess whether the ambulance drivers will turn right or left."

It doesn't have to be this way and I have some patients who thoroughly enjoy the retirement center, but they are a small handful and I suspect they enjoy themselves in spite of the surroundings.

A survey was taken of several thousand doctors to see where they planned to retire. Not one was planning to move to a retirement center. Let's take a closer look. Why are so many retired people leaving their familiar surroundings, selling their life possessions and moving across town or across the country to a retirement center or as one patient puts it, "a nursing home with individual cottages?" On the surface the obvious reason is to move to a "friendly place where life really begins" as one advertisement clearly states. I haven't heard a single elderly patient put it this way.

"We're tired of paying taxes for schools, our kids are grown; we've had it with the dogs and kids running through our yard; we don't want to keep a large yard and home anymore; some undesirables were moving into our area; we don't have a single minority group in the whole complex now; on Halloween the pranksters don't even get by the guards at the front gate, we don't have to buy a single treat."

To me this list is more of a getaway than a get-to. The end result is that we are "getting away" from all the things that were keeping us going. If we remove all these activities and the work and attention that they require, we're going to be left with a big empty sack unless we replace them with something equally consuming. Herein lies the problem.

I have one 78-year-old lady who says it much better than I can. She had just returned from a trip to Hawaii with a smile that really pulled her face apart.

"Doctor, we've had the time of our lives. I've celebrated my 78th birthday and it was truly the happiest day of my life, the nicest birthday I ever had."

My curiosity was up. "How did you celebrate?" I asked.

"We spent a relaxing day and then had a birthday party on the beach with a family of Hawaiians that we had gotten to know over the years. We had a luau and afterwards all of the children and teenagers played their ukeleles and serenaded me until long after midnight. I had never had a more enjoyable evening and I'll remember it all of my life," she said.

I didn't say much, just smiled in my confusion. Here was a lady relating how children had presented her with the most wonderful day of her life and she came back to live in a community where children needed a "Visitor's Pass" to get in. Where guards patrol on Halloween, where children can't swim in the pool with their grandparents. Where if the shrubs get over a designated height, the neighbors notify the management and they get promptly trimmed down. Where life begins? I doubt it.

I've told elderly patients who come in all upset about the

retirement center, their health and life in general, that old people just aren't that exciting. Before they can leap out of their chairs I explain that children or middle-aged people aren't that exciting either, when placed alone. It's the mixture of all ages that makes life interesting. We need the interchange of ideas; the spontaneity of youth's curiosity; the struggles and victories of middle-age; the wisdom and seasoning of the elderly. When you toss all these ingredients in the pot, you end up with a glorious stew. Separate the ingredients and you rapidly lose the flavor.

I had the good fortune to be a "house boy" for an elderly architect and his wife when I was in pre-medical studies at the university. They were a lovely older pair and became second parents to me. He was the most brilliant man I ever met and she taught me more psychology than I ever learned at medical school.

She told me, "Don, if you ever get to the point where you feel that youth is all bad, you're in real trouble. You're getting old fast."

She was right and lived her words. The last time we were in Omaha, Carolyn and I went to a convalescent home to see her. She had aged of course and had lost some of her sparkle and was having some trouble with her memory. We had a nice chat and as we were ready to leave I asked her if there was anything I could do or get for her.

"No, nothing I guess. I have all I need, thanks so much for coming and tell Pam and Sue 'Hi' for me," she said.

We were nearly at the door, when she hollered, "Yes, there is one thing if it wouldn't be too much trouble. These are such exciting times to live in. Would you please keep me posted of any new discoveries in the medical field? I just have to keep up with the world."

"These are such exciting times." How can you lose with an attitude like that? You can't! It doesn't matter where you're living if you can hold on to that approach to life. All I'm saying is it's harder to hold on to this approach if you're surrounded by people who didn't have it or have lost it. As one lady told me: "It's darned hard to whistle 'Oh, what a beautiful morning' when the first three people I run into tell me what their bowels have done in the past 24 hours."

In the shadow of security, control is usually lurking. If we control who our neighbors are going to be by an age limit; if we control our yards by giving allowable heights for shrubs and plants; if we control who can visit our community by issuing "Visitors' Passes," we are controlling life itself.

Robert Lewis Stevenson said, "To forego all the issues of living in a parlor with a regulated temperature, as if that were not to die a hundred times over, and for ten years at a stretch! As if it were not to die in one's own lifetime, and without even the sad immunities of death! As if it were not to die, and yet be the patient spectators of our own pitiable change! It is better to lose health like a spendthrift than to waste it like a miser. It is better to live and be done with it, than to die daily in the sickroom."

At a conference on self-care, one of the most talented speakers was from a major eastern university. He had a severe physical handicap, and walked with a cane, due to polio at an earlier age. He gave an interesting talk about health from a sociological point of view, and near the end of his speech he lashed out at the audience for advising everyone (but mainly him) to quit smoking. He said:

"I am interested in the quality of life, not the quantity. I enjoy smoking. I use cigarettes in moderation, and they add enjoyment to my life. What kind of years are you doctors offering me? If you are going to prolong my life so that I can get an extra ten years in a nursing home, forget it. I am not interested in those years. I'm only interested in the quality of my years, not the quantity. Don't offer me more years with my pleasures removed. I'm worried about this awesome power of doctors."

He felt the same as Stevenson. He wants to live and be done with it, in his own fashion.

We tend to form what we feel is a protective shell with aging. Actually, it is a destructive shell. The result is that we seal ourselves off from the world both mentally and physically. We get more concerned about finances, the deplorable state of our youth, and the world in general. We become obsessed with our health, and for what reason; to be able to stay hard at work erecting our shell.

One elderly patient called me to her home, because she was short of breath. I found her in mild congestive heart failure. She needed hospitalization to receive oxygen and to get rid of some excess fluid in her lungs and her body in general. She was very wealthy and was most concerned about getting her diamonds and cash gathered up: she said she had about $40,000 in cash on hand that she hadn't deposited that week. She refused to go to the hospital until she and her attorney could work things out. The next afternoon she agreed to go to the hospital. Her attorney had "taken care of" the cash, and her fingers glistened with the precious stones.

That same day I admitted another elderly lady to the hospital, one had who suffered a slight stroke. She had no attorney, no diamonds, and was barely getting by on Social Security. My daily rounds to those two patients taught me much about our protective shells. The poor lady with the stroke had so many visitors I could hardly get into her room to check her. They were dear friends, and I had trouble asking them to step outside for a minute. Her room was overflowing with flowers.

But "Mrs. Rich's" room was different. Her only flowers came from the attorney, who spent a good part of each afternoon and evening with her. He was her only visitor during her two week stay in the hospital. My curiosity got the best of me, and I checked with the floor nurses. They said the contrast between these two rooms was truly unbelievable. One had the most secure financial and legal protective shell money could buy. The other patient couldn't afford a protective shell and didn't need one. What she had was an open path to her heart, and her numerous friends used it daily.

Retirement can be especially unbearable if we "escaped" to our job all our life. I'm not impressed with people whose jobs "consume" them. It's the other way around; they consume the job.

The newspaper recently featured a "citizen of the year" type of businessman who was moving away. I counted his triumphs. He was the head of 12 different civic and business organizations. How can you run your own business and head 11 more and have any time for a family? You can't.

Frequently the wife is equally "civic minded." This completes the noble family, loaded with do-good ambitions for the world. I don't think so. I see two people who are loaded with boredom and frustration in their relationship with each other and who will do anything to devise ways of keeping distance between them. The stress of the civic and business activities is a lot less than the stress of being trapped in the same room for 30 minutes with each other. Retire from both our job, and our activities and we're on thin ice with hot feet.

Robert Browning said, "The last of life, for which the first was made." The last of life will be *AS* the first was made. So we have to start making it worthwhile now.

We have to enjoy ourselves along the way. We have to have some "fun time" as well as "profit time." We have to learn to enjoy ourselves and each other. In retirement we have to have "profit time" as well as "fun time." We can't have it all fun time or we'll feel unproductive and surely wither. African Violets and wood carving are fine, but don't give them all away. Most people will praise the works of charity. Few would pay for them under a different label. The deduction is obvious. Your creations are wonderful, considering the price. Find an outlet for your products, put a price tag on them, see if they are so good. If not, find out why and get to work. It will mean a lot more to your well being.

Carolyn, my wife, doesn't agree with this theory. She tells me she knows what I am trying to say, but "it sounds commercial, and that is not you." We've argued the point, and maybe it is being "commercial," but that is the way I see it. I think charity is great in the right setting, but I've seen too many persons trying to help themselves by doing part or full time charitable work. I see this as being another "tax deduction" type of giving all too often. Are we trying to give something, or get something? For some it works out, but I see too many patients who've tried who are unfulfilled with this existence. They seem to get the message that most things of value in this world have a price tag, including jobs. The most common picture I see is the woman who loses her husband and decides to occupy her time and give of herself by being a full time hospital volunteer. It works occasionally, but not for the majority. Usually such a woman doesn't need to "occupy" herself, she needs to "fulfill" herself. She can't afford to give much more, and she needs to receive something at a time like this. She needs a feeling of worth in the world more than ever and she'll come a lot closer to it with a paycheck and helpful criticism than she will with "Thank you, what would we do without you?" An hour or two or a day a week of charity may be fine, but I haven't observed it work as a career.

Giving away all your creative works is in the same category. Surprising a friend with a creation can be very rewarding, but make it a policy and you soon lose perspective concerning your work. Take Henry, a 90-year-old patient of mine, for example. Henry has been painting with oils for years. He's had some lessons, and does a fair amateurish job. Everyone has been given one of his paintings, and the work always is accepted with praise and adulation. Henry is even asked to put on showings here and there, at a bank or a neighborhood gallery. In effect the bank or gallery get free wall coverings for a week or so.

But how is the artist doing? He's a delightful man, but he's very depressed:

"Everyone loves my pictures, Doctor, but I never have sold a one. I get so upset. Why do people ask me to pack them up and bring them down for a hanging, and then never contact me again? I go back a few weeks later and all my paintings are stacked up and someone else's pictures are up. I haven't painted a thing in a year and a half. Why should I? What's the use any more?"

Well, is this commercialism? I don't think so. Henry doesn't need the money, but he does need the feeling of worth he's not getting. He wants his pictures to sell like those of other artists: then he'll know "people like them." He's been cruelly misled, yet he's done it to himself. If he had just put a price tag on them years ago he would have gotten the message and could have continued to improve until they did sell or tried another field for his creativity.

As one of my long-time artist friends in Omaha says:

"Don't tell me I paint pretty pictures. I'll know you think so

116

when you buy one." And people do, at $1,000 apiece. And, he's not depressed!

Retirement can be fun. I see many patients having the time of their lives. These are the ones who have been living life to the fullest the last fifty or sixty years, and who won't get all their plans completed if they live to be 100. Living can't be put off for that wonderful "someday." We can't wait for that day when we get the engraved gold watch from the company to "begin to live." Too many hours have ticked away by then.

9 - Isn't Anyone Going To Start Talking?

I recently had a long conversation with one of my neurologist friends. We were discussing a patient of mine who was in the hospital and I had asked him to see her in consultation. The patient had me a bit confused. I had "inherited" her from a retired doctor who had prescribed numerous medications: codeine, valium, tylenol, rectal suppositories for nausea and sedation, hormones, thyroid tablets, diuretics — you name it, she was taking it. I tried to slowly wean her from some of her medications but with little success.

"I tried to go three days without my valium and look at me. I am a shaking wreck." And she was.

"Okay, we'll stay on it," I said, "but you're going to have to gradually cut down." I couldn't get her to reveal a single problem. Everything was just great. Great except for headaches, dizziness, fainting, stomach aches and diarrhea. There was nothing left for surgery. She had had 9 major operations at age 44. I admitted her to the hospital after she had passed out at home. She was clear at times and semi-comatose the rest of the time. After numerous examinations and tests we decided her medication had simply caught up with her. As it turned out, two other doctors had been prescribing medications for her at the same time. Her husband told me that her prescriptions alone were running well over $100.00 a month!

The neurologist and I both were concerned after the diagnosis became clear. We really didn't diagnose her case, she just got better each day as she excreted a few more chemicals (including those I had prescribed) from her body. The neurologist and I had a cup of coffee and a longer than usual discussion about the patient and her problem. Then he asked me:

"Don, isn't anyone going to start talking? Doesn't anyone have time to start leveling with patients like this? She doesn't need my services as a neurologist — she needs someone to talk to and iron out some problems. You guys out in general practice can't do it, I know. I try to send families to you, and they call back and say 'Dr. Fisher isn't taking any more patients.' I see this all the time. The patients end up at my door for help, and I really don't have anything to offer them. I do all the tests, and nothing ever shows. Then I don't know what to tell them. They are grasping at straws for me to diagnose and cure their problem. They're lined up in my office for brain scans and electroencephalograms. They want the works. All I can think of is, 'Where could I send this patient so that somehow he could begin to talk and work out the problem?' But I honestly don't know where to start. I end up adding a different colored pill, and we're right back where we started. We've got to stop all this somehow; we've got to slow down, someone has got to start talking."

He's basically right, but what he really means is "someone has got to start listening." We've all forgotten how to listen. Especially in the medical field. Casual listening may be okay at the cocktail party or at work, but in the doctor's office or in the hospital it can be and often is tragic.

The neurologist didn't stop there. He added, "You know, nine times out of ten the patient will tell us what's wrong if we'll just listen. We can't keep on testing with more dangerous and more expensive tests until the patient gets mad and goes somewhere else and starts over."

The disturbing thing to me is that we aren't even headed in the right direction. We've gotten so far ahead of ourselves technically that we will never catch up practically and philosophically unless we stop looking to the next technical advance and start dusting off some of the old, proven principles.

It's a bit like the farmer who was asked by the county extension agent why he didn't come to any of the meetings to hear some of the newer ideas about farming. The farmer replied, "Hell, I ain't farming now half as good as I know how."

That's our position. We aren't treating ourselves "half as good as we know how." It's mutual. Both the doctor and the patient are at fault. You and I are demanding a pain-free healthful utopia to age 95 and scientists are trying to promise it. If I have a problem, someone had better fix it fast.

One elderly patient came in with a variety of symptoms all of which were most likely attributable to her advancing years. She had been seen by several doctors and had been given an assortment of prescriptions to get her on her way, none of which had worked. After examining her I pulled myself together and in a brave moment said, "I'm afraid most of these symptoms are simply due to your age and there isn't a lot to do for them."

She sighed and sat back in her chair with a big grin. "Doctor, that helps so much to know. I was worried it could be something else more serious and none of the others really told me what it was. I can accept that and adjust to it now that I know what is causing it. I guess I should expect some aches and pains at my age."

I recently asked the director of our medical society what complaints he heard most often about doctors.

"That's easy," he said, "lack of communication is number one; a touch of compassion would help in the second complaint area." He felt our malpractice problems would be sharply reduced if doctors started listening and talking and started showing a "touch of compassion." Remember he's on our side, a paid representative; he's not an outside critic. If that's the way he sees it, maybe physicians had better listen.

The problem really comes into focus if our thoughts so far are right. If 75 percent of our illnesses are due to emotions and no one is talking or listening, we're on a dead end road! This is why this book is directed to the "lay" audience. If doctors aren't tuned in to the emotional or psychosomatic side of medicine, the patient has got to be. But even if every physican in this country "tuned in" it wouldn't solve all the problems when we consider that we have over 200 million people in this country and less than 200 thousand total doctors seeing patients in active office practice.

Statistics show that almost 20 million people in the United States suffer from depression. There are 20,000 psychiatrists. The psychiatrists and psychoanalysts can't begin to treat this volume of patients. The logical conclusion is that the family physician must become "psychologically oriented." The bothersome fact is that most physicians aren't "psychologically oriented" and hence we're not even coming close to treating the cases of depression alone.

So, the problem begins to sound hopeless, doesn't it? It's not unless we keep on our rocket-paced course seeking complex technical answers to simple problems that we are causing to ourselves. Researchers are looking for hundreds of new ways to treat heart disease. More and more heart surgery is being done, the push is on. But no one is saying, "Hold it. What's causing all this? Why are so many 30-and 40-year-old men ending up in the obituary columns?" Whatever happened to that Biblical promise of three-score and ten years, or were there conditions attached that I have missed: only if you jog 10 miles a day; don't smoke; don't eat cholesterol; don't become overweight. And I don't think the good Lord had a coronary bypass at age 40 in mind.

I recently heard a cardiac surgeon say, "Coronary bypass results so far do not convince me that we are altering the natural course of the disease." Yet it's the popular thing to do. Full steam ahead. We're now doing 75,000 coronary bypass operations a year in this country and we're not even sure it's beneficial. One recent study asks, "Is the anginal relief that occurs and persists after bypass surgery due to a long-term placebo effect?" The answer, surprisingly enough, is yes in a significant number of cases according to an internationally recognized authority. Dr. Lucien Campeau, chief of cardiology at Montreal Cardiologic Institute, found that in 235 bypass patients, as many as 50 percent of the patients whose grafts had failed at three years follow-up reported their angina was improved and that half of these patients were angina free. He felt that the most plausible explanation for their relief of pain was most likely due to decreased weight loss, less strenuous work, cessation of cigarette smoking, decreased anxiety following surgery and improved medical therapy. In other words, even though the medical surgery was not successful the patients improved because of changes they made *after* surgery. If most of the benefits are going to be derived from changes we make in our lifestyle after surgery, I think it's time we look for a less hazardous and less expensive placebo.

I'm sure that exercise, overweight, excessive cholesterol, and smoking are contributing factors, but only in relation to the person's state of mind. That's why all of the studies have been so confusing. We have one group saying cholesterol will surely kill you and another group saying it's a necessary chemical for the manufacture of sexual hormones and has no bearing on heart disease. Apparently it's a matter of how you want to go.

One internationally famous cardiologist recently laughed at the whole cholesterol story as related to heart disease. He scoffed at the worry over cholesterol blood levels and had plenty of evidence to show that lowering the cholesterol did not equate with longevity. He was 60 pounds overweight, close to his promised 70 years and he ate enough cholesterol laden hors d'oeuvres after the lecture to convince us he was serious!

He is right to a point. In other words, if you are at peace with yourself and have it "going for you" you can probably eat all the cholesterol you want, let someone else do the jogging for you while you smoke a cigar and probably live out your promised time. I have followed numerous patients who have borne this out. They've done nearly everything wrong, but not quite. They kept life in perspective; they didn't "pick the leaves from the trees."

One patient of mine portrays this exceptionally well. The first time Arthur waddled in he was 66-years-old and in sad shape to my way of thinking, not his. He was markedly overweight and an alcoholic's alcoholic. His cholesterol level was a staggering 800 milligrams percent (normal 150-300), his liver would have filled a parking lot and he was severely anemic with a hemoglobin of 6 (normal is 14). He brought his beer home each week in a pickup truck, the back end. The interesting thing is Arthur didn't come in, his wife sent him in for me to work miracles.

I asked him, "Do you drink much, Art?"

"Nah, Doc, I spill most of it," he chortled. I tried in my most naive way to show him the light. Arthur tolerated my sermon. I got as far as the mission worker on skid road who propped up a drunk and gave him a little demonstration. She had a jar of water and a jar of alcohol. She took out a worm and placed it in a jar of water. "See how the worm thrives in the water," she said. Then she put the worm in the jar of alcohol and it died.

"Now," she said, "what do you conclude from this?"

The drunk looked up and proudly said, "Well, I know I'll never have worms." That was Arthur.

I pointed out his low blood count, his enlarged liver and his high cholesterol. I told him either stop drinking or he wouldn't be around long. He needed hospitalization but wouldn't consider it. His wife sent him back two years later, no better and no worse. This time he had all the same findings plus one more. He had an elevated blood sugar indicating diabetes. I hated to add this to his existing health disasters, but I had to do it.

I marched in with a sad face, "Art, I hate to tell you this, but now you have diabetes."

"Diabetes," he questioned with a gaping grin, "isn't that the one where you get a card that says, I'm not intoxicated, I'm a diabetic?"

"That's the one, Art," I replied, unbelievingly.

He patted me on the shoulder and strolled out with a handful of instructions that I'm sure he put in the back of the pickup with the weekly beer supply.

He quit coming and his wife told me he found a doctor who had an occasional drink with him and that he is now doing great. He lived 12 more years and died at age 78. I don't know what finally brought him down but I'm sure he didn't die worrying about himself or picking the leaves from the trees. His lack of anxiety helped him get 12 years that I didn't feel he'd have.

I'm not saying that overeating, overdrinking and oversmoking is the way to eternal health. We can get lost in details and forget the main issue of how we're facing life. I think our attitude is much more important than what we're eating or drinking. And, it naturally follows, if our attitude is "okay" we'll handle the incidentals okay, too.

I was shopping in one of our large bookstores one day when an old man came up to me and said, "Say, I see you're smoking a pipe. I just got in all kinds of trouble with my doctor about my smoking. How old do you think I am?"

I looked at him and before I could answer he said, "Ninety-three, and my doctor says if I don't quit smoking he's going to quit taking care of me. He says it's wrecking my health and he can't help me with my blood pressure if I don't stop smoking."

"How much do you smoke," I asked.

"Three cigarettes a day. I always have for the last 40 years," he said.

Three cigarettes a day and that's killing him at age 93? He was so upset and shaking that the biggest threat to his health was worrying about losing his doctor. It reminded me of an old antique pipe rack a nurse of mine gave me years ago. It had a layer of dirt and grime on it and after I cleaned it off I could read "He who does not smoke has either known no great grief or refuseth himself the softest consolation next to that which comes from heaven."

One of the reasons that prevents doctors from talking or listening is that we're afraid of the answers we'll get. What do we do if the patient opens up and hands us this problem. We can't treat it with a pill and that stops too many doctors. As one colleague says, "I always give the patients a few prescriptions, because that's what they come in for." Should patients come in to get prescriptions, or should they come in to get well?

I had one patient with a persistent ringing in his ears. He was 55-years-old and I felt it was the usual problem which is felt to be due to a circulatory problem in the small blood vessels of the ear for which nothing or little can be done. It bothered him a great deal and I felt he should see a specialist. The ear specialist placed him on a small medication to dilate the arteries in the ear and released him. He came back a few months later and said the medication had not helped. He asked to be referred to another ear specialist. I felt it would not be helpful but at his urging gave him another name. He came back one year later with the same complaint and said he had received no help from the second specialist. He insisted on seeing one more and I reluctantly went along.

He came back all in smiles. "That doctor is great. If I or my family ever have an ear problem, we're going back to him. I'd recommend him to anyone," he said.

"Really," I asked. "What did he do?"

"He told me there wasn't a damned thing to do for it. That really helped to get an answer."

Someone was talking!

Talking is only part of it. We're having as much trouble, if not more, listening to people. I mean really listening, not just hearing words. We're all too busy getting our answer ready, or judging the other person's statement to really listen. I know I'm guilty. I know I'm forming answers when I should be "plugged in." I know the patients are guilty, too. I know they get things all twisted because they're thinking of the next question when they should be listening.

Several studies have been done in which the patient-doctor conversation has been recorded. The patient was interviewed a short while later to see how much he or she had retained of the original study. In one study only ten percent of the patients could remember being told of any surgical complications that might arise from the operation. It would have been equally interesting to check the doctors to see how much they remembered about what the patients told them.

My point is this. If we can't start to talk and listen, why keep pushing for more technical breakthroughs? What would we do if we found one? The biggest medical breakthrough we can possibly achieve is to learn to get across to each other. This is where we ought to be putting our efforts. Once we have mastered the basics then we can speed on to the scientific breakthroughs. Then we will be able to use them.

A recent medical article stated that the fear of cancer, or cancerophobia in this country is worse than the disease. It described the wide fear of cancer and the anxiety we all have. The author felt that this was a greater threat to our health than cancer itself.

One 9-year-old boy came in, because his mother had noted his "glands were swollen" in his neck. I examined him and found that he had tonsillitis, with the usual swollen lymph glands under his jaw. But, after I had checked his throat and felt his glands, he looked up at me and said in a serious tone:

"Doctor, if I have cancer, I'll shoot myself."

Nine years old!

I frequently see this in practice. I once was examining a 60-year-old man and was feeling his neck and thyroid gland. I asked him to swallow.

"Swollen," he screamed, and leaped off the table.

I reassured him I had said to "swallow" — not "swollen". He broke out in a sweat and began to shake. The underlying fear and panic was near the surface. He's living with the fear of anything being swollen 24 hours a day. If he has anything to fear, it's fear itself. My neurologist friend wants us to start talking for a reason. He's in a field where few definite diagnoses are made. As he says, "I do all the tests; I have to. That's what the patients have been sent in for. But they're nearly always normal. If a new test comes along, I'd better darned well do it. It doesn't matter what the cost or the danger to the patient. The patient, the family and the referring doctor want the works."

The neurologist is frustrated like me and a lot of you. He wants us to start talking. If someone had been talking the patient wouldn't be knocking at his door with complaints of arm or leg numbness, headaches, fainting, weakness, etc. He's saying that talking would have prevented problems that he can't cure. He's frustrated, because he "can't talk" and doesn't know where to send the patient. He has people lined up for electroencephalographs, sonic brain tests, spinal taps, and lengthy reports to dictate.

Often it is the patient or a relative who demands the test. A lady called me at the office one morning and said, "Doctor, my husband woke up with a headache. I want you to schedule a complete body scan at the hospital today." She didn't want any advice, just the latest in scientific testing.

Hospitals and clinics are adding expensive new devices constantly, and let's face it: if they make the investment in a half-million dollar piece of equipment such as a body scanner, you can be sure they are going to want to use it often. As this book is being written, a law suit is going on in a southern state where a hospital and an adjacent clinic installed body scanners, at great expense to both. What has brought them to the courts is the question of which one gets to do the body scans on mutual clinic and hospital patients. Is this good medicine, or good business?

I had a call one morning from a middle aged man who was completely upset.

"It's my wife," he said, "and I guess it's me, too. She needs to see you badly. She's dizzy and has been for two weeks over the Christmas holidays. You know she had 'that thing' 16 years ago in Illinois, maybe she's never mentioned it to you. The doctors mentioned MS (Multiple Sclerosis). It haunts her and frankly it haunts me, too. We saw all the best doctors and had every kind of test. One doctor said he 'wouldn't cast a vote either way.' The last doctor, a neurologist, called it a 'bizarre neurological happening.' We had a minister we thought a great deal of; you know, a rare person who could make us believe she would get well. He got her and me both straightened out."

A rare person who could make us believe she could get well. Wouldn't it be nice if that kind of person wasn't so rare. And wouldn't it be nice if one of the doctors had displayed a touch of this or at least "cast a vote" in her favor instead of letting her dangle with a "bizzare neurological happening" for 16 years.

She didn't have MS. She had a house full of company for the holidays, three children home from college, an elderly father-in-law and a distant cousin. She spent the last 15 years bringing her mother home with her when her mother's neighbors called and said, "She's depressed, drinking again, and she's not eating. She misses you so, you'll have to come and get her." Try all this on for size and you and I would be dizzy too, especially with a bizarre neurological happening in our past. She broke down crying after I told her she had no symptoms of MS.

"I really didn't think so, but the seed was planted, now I'll always wonder. They never told me if it was or wasn't. I think if I could solve the problem with mother, I'd be okay. When I had my first dizzy spell we had just moved across the country to Chicago; my husband was starting a job with a new firm; we had just bought a new house and had not sold our old one in Maryland and we had six different sets of house guests the first two months we were there. I always wondered if that couldn't have done it. No one asked about it so I felt it wasn't important."

After seeing her I reviewed the literature on Multiple

Sclerosis. I was curious to see if emotions were even being considered as a cause. I've had three patients with Multiple Sclerosis who definitely feel they can name a specific emotion that triggered their MS and pinpoint the time it started.

One mother pointed to a two-year-old girl and said, "It started the day we brought her home from the hospital. My husband and I didn't really know each other. We had our own problems and we weren't ready for her." She may be right.

Regarding MS, Cecil & Loeb, a standard textbook of medicine states: "corrective psychotherapy, more properly the function of the psychiatrist, aims at a profound reorganization of the personality for the release of anxiety, hostility and resentment and the stimulation of emotional maturation in growth, in this way perhaps influencing the progress of the disease."

I can't help wonder that if a profound reorganization of the personality will influence the progress of the disease, would preventing the disorganization of the personality in the first place prevent the disease?

Another patient swears his symptoms started the day he was promoted to a job he couldn't stand in a corporation he wanted to leave. The third patient is an attractive lady who developed the onsets of her disease shortly after her husband confessed to having an affair. She is a nurse, and in her mind there is no doubt about the cause of her disease.

So who do we start talking and listening to? Ourselves and each other. We can't all do it in the doctor's office. There just isn't enough time, money or doctors to go around. We're going to have to do this on our own with our family and friends.

I think it would be worth forming a neighborhood club just to meet and talk once a week or even once a month. It may sound dull, but it would be a start. Oregon had a severe flood in 1964 and our entire neighborhood was completely flooded. We all lost thousands of dollars worth of household goods. After the cleanup we got together to talk about ways of handling "high water" if it ever came again. After the meeting several neighbors down the lane came up to me and said the flood almost was worth it, just to spend a night getting together!

Maybe we've lost something along the way. Maybe we'd do better if we didn't have insurance and if someone had a fire or storm loss we all pitched in to help rebuild. Maybe the old barn raising days offered something missing from society now. Maybe we'd better get back to ground zero. I will always remember the "October 12 storm" in Portland. Many patients came in the following days complaining of their losses — of cars being wrecked by trees, of trees falling across roofs, etc. But the complaints had a strange ring to them. They all were sorry that more damage had not been done, that the car hadn't been totaled, that the living room hadn't been crushed by the tree, too, so it could be remodeled. Not one person complained about the actual loss they had suffered. It rather confused me. It seems we've even forgotten how to interpret a loss.

Once we start talking and listening we won't have to dial a "Suicide Prevention" number. We're always shocked about a suicide in the neighborhood. Why would he or she do it? They seemed so happy just a few days before. A patient came in upset, because her best friend had just shot herself a few days before Christmas. She committed suicide and left her husband and several small children.

"I was with her a few days before and she seemed so happy. She was planning to take some courses at a Community College and was all excited about it," she said.

What happened? We don't know. Of course we're shocked. If anyone had been talking or listening, it wouldn't have been such a surprise. If any of us were talking, really talking, we'd know what our best friend was thinking. We would know that our wife or husband or child or friend was at the depths of despair and couldn't go on. How pathetic, two good friends talk a few days before suicide and everything's "neat" and "great," or "fantastic" and "cool."

It's the same with a murder or other violent crime. How could he or she do it. They couldn't do such a thing. Oh, no? They just wiped out the family they loved. Everyone knows they were the ideal close-knit family. Always kept to themselves and never bothered anyone. The pride of the community. We see it all the time. Here's a father, mother or child that snuffs out the family and no one believes it. Here's all this love that has been turning to a violent hatred and no one even suspects it. Things were just "great" the day before. You and I can't buy that.

We can't "plug in" to each other's minds, but we can come a lot closer than we are doing now. We can start sending a lot better signals back and forth than we have been. We can quit being "great" when we're at the end of the line. We can be in rough shape and let someone know it. That's when help arrives. Try it. We can't tell the wife who's lost her husband or the family who's lost a child to "come on now, get back in the groove, it's time to stick your chin up, time will cure." Time won't cure it, it will cushion it, but it won't cure it and the one with the loss doesn't need that approach. They need to hear, "It's rough, the loss was terrific, and you're bound to be down. It's hell I know, but we're right alongside to help in anyway that we can." There's an important point here. We're letting them have their loss. If we start telling someone to "get with it, act tough" we're not listening. We're denying the tragedy happened. Who's going to tell us how it is with them if we cut them off at the "emotional pass."

I had one patient come in quite upset after losing her husband. She was quite distraught, because all of her friends told her the mourning period was over and she should get with it and quit feeling sorry for herself. She is better, as far as her friends know. She tells them she's just fine and things couldn't be better, which is all they want to hear. Now if she takes an overdose of sleeping pills some night, they'll all be shocked. She was "doing so well."

Not opening our hearts and discussing our thoughts can kill us, literally. Two cases will always haunt me.

I had one 19-year-old girl who was unmarried and pregnant. I delivered her and she and the baby did fine for two days. Then she became ill with a loss of appetite and developed a rapid heartbeat. I thought I had missed a rheumatic heart defect, but could hear no murmurs. I had a cardiologist and an internist see her and nothing could be diagnosed except a critically ill young mother.

In a weak voice she finally told me on the third day "I know what's wrong. I'm so ashamed to be in the Maternity Ward with all these married mothers."

I transferred her to the general hospital next door and she began to do better. I had just left her on the fifth day and she looked fine and checked normal. When I got to the office the hospital had called and said that she "had just expired." The autopsy was eagerly awaited, but it gave no clues.

The second one was a 54-year-old lady who came in, because of fainting spells. Her husband called me aside and told me his thoughts.

"She's been upset every since we drove down and saw our son-in-law and daughter and the four grandchildren. The kids aren't happy out here and have been talking about moving back to Tennessee. We thought we had talked them out of it until we pulled into the yard and saw that damned 'FOR SALE' sign. Pat got sick right then and there and made me turn around and drive all the way back home. She wouldn't even get out of the car she was so upset, even though we had driven 100 miles to see them. We can't even talk about it."

Pat began to look worse and began to run a fever and to lose weight. Her condition deteriorated rapidly and I hospitalized her. She continued to go downhill in the hospital and the consultants and I thought she must have a hidden malignancy, so an exploratory operation was done. Everything was normal. All of her laboratory tests were normal. She improved somewhat after the surgery, but began to worsen three weeks later back home. She was readmitted and proceeded to die without even the benefit of a diagnosis. Her husband and I had our own diagnosis, but there was "nothing to bandage." The autopsy again revealed only the terminal changes expected at death.

No one was talking and no one was listening.

I could only think of Voltaire's words: "Doctors are men who prescribe medicine of which they know little, to cure diseases of which they know less, and in human beings of whom they know nothing."

Try talking and listening to at least one good friend tomorrow. See how hard it is. We're all out of practice. Forget the national chant "have a good day." Your dog will do that without even being reminded. And don't "communicate." You can do that with your radio, television set or newspaper. The word has been sadly beaten to death. Talk and listen.

If you can't trap a friend and are desperate, try it with a family member. Bring up a sensitive subject like religion, love, communism, divorce, anything with an emotional ring to it. See if you can actually listen to someone, really hear their viewpoint without preparing a judgment at the same time. See if you can understand what and why they're feeling and saying. You don't have to agree or disagree or pass judgment. Judgments are made in the courtroom and most people can't wait to leave one.

It's the same with children. If Freddie comes home and says he wants to quit the paper route, how are you going to handle it?

"I don't care what you want, son, you'll need the money for college. I want you to learn the value of a dollar. Someday you'll be glad I made you stick to it."

Or, "Let's talk about it. What kind of problems are you having with the paper route?" With the latter approach you'll keep the channels open and you'll keep them open for the next problem that arises. There might be a new family on the street with a dog the size of Bigfoot that breathes like a dragon on parade day. He may need help from dad or the dogcatcher. He may be just tired or lazy (your worst suspicion) but you'll never know if you don't hear him out.

Once the channels are shut down they're awfully hard to open, and most likely they're closed for good!

We've got to keep a close check on our circle of friends so we have someone to share ideas with. As Emerson said, "Go often to the house of thy friend, for weeds choke the unused path." Some days I wouldn't make it without friends like Chuck South, Bob Kalez, Dave Butler and Tom Reid. Our books and hobbies and various interests are fine, but they're still not human beings. Remember, solitary confinement is still called the cruelest punishment. As Martin Buber said, "I knew nothing of books when I came forth from the womb of my mother and I shall die without books, with another human hand in my own. I do, indeed, close my door at times and surrender myself to a book, but only because I can open the door again and see another human being looking at me."

10 – He Who Laughs, Lasts

He or she who laughs, lasts longer. In fact, next to the long, happy marriage most of my older patients tell me is the number one key to their success, they rate humor as a close second. They say it in a variety of ways.

"We don't take life too seriously."

"We're able to throw things off."

"We pick ourselves up fast."

"We're able to laugh at ourselves and the world."

"Why worry about life you can't control it anyway."

They're all saying the same thing in different words. Maybe a sense of humor isn't the right term and we can call it what we like, but if you're going to take life light-hearted, throw things off, and pick yourself up fast you've got to have a twinkle in your eye or a chuckle near the surface.

I questioned adding a chapter about humor but the more I thought about it the more fitting I felt it was. If humor is important to so many of my patients in maintaining their health and happiness, we'd better see how it works.

I've used humor daily in practice since my opening day and I'm sure it's cushioned many and otherwise impossible moments. I've been able to laugh at and with patients and they with me. I have never seen a case or a diagnosis where the ability to laugh didn't add something. If there is one prescription I would write for a universal cure-all, it would be the ability to see the amusing side of things.

I think some physicians are afraid of any levity, because it gets them "down to patient level." If a doctor begins to smile or laugh with patients at their and his foibles, he's going to appear human and may lose something. It removes the formal authoritarian base that too many physicians need. Numerous patients have come in saying that they were "changing doctors because he was good, but he seemed so serious all the time." As one patient said, "It was bad enough to know I had heart trouble without him being so serious and stern." In the study I mentioned earlier in which patients were asked the complaints they had about doctors, they said that they would like to see doctors "smile" more often. They have a good case.

One of the speakers at a recent mental health symposium I attended was a "Dr. Sober" himself, a psychiatrist. He was so solemn and serious that one of his associates at the medical school asked him during the question session, "Do you feel a sense of humor has any place in psychiatry?" He didn't get the jibe, or maybe he did – we couldn't tell.

130

"Oh, no," he replied sternly. "I see no place for humor in medicine at all, and least of all not in psychiatry. I don't see how we could employ levity in any of these tragic problems we're confronted with. Possibly that's why I went into academic medicine, to teach, I don't know. I do know that I would never use it if I was seeing patients in private practice." Thank goodness he's not.

I disagree. We need all the levity we can get to make these tragic problems seem less tragic. The collection boxes for tragedies and comedies are placed too close together and it is easy to drop our situation into the wrong box. One of our major problems, I feel, is that we have trouble remembering how to laugh. It's a bit suggestive to me that one of the hottest selling items recently has been the "SMILE" button or "smile sticker." It's a little different really, if you want to see a happy face, you buy some smile stickers and plaster them everywhere. It may be a start in the right direction, but you and I can do a lot better with a real smile.

The author of an editorial in a national magazine not long ago felt that the wave of Polish jokes was damaging all Eastern European people in general. He felt that being the butt of "dumb Polack" jokes was degrading and tended to expose "deep self-doubts" of the Polish people. He felt that anti-defamation societies should join in protest against people who tell such ethnic jokes. Yet in the same article he states that ethnic humor is one of the great assets of the nation!

Ethnic humor is more than an asset. It is vital, along with all the other jokes we're not telling! To me it's a lot better being the butt of any "joke" than not being joked at all. The Polish people have to be the luckiest group of people in this decade. When you have the whole world joking about you, you know you're special and have what it takes. If you want to really ruin someone you do it, but you don't joke about it. It's the "ethnic groups" that aren't being joked about that have need for concern.

It's the same with individuals and I think we should be able to laugh at someone as well as with them, contrary to what we were taught. Jack Benny was the butt of countless jokes and endeared himself to millions in the process. His "self-doubts" exposure is what made the world love him. The quickest way to expose our self-doubts is to quit laughing about them.

As one patient put it, "I like to put myself down before others get a chance, that way *I* get the punch line."

John Masefield in his famous poem, "Sea Fever," said, "And all I ask is a merry yarn from a laughing fellow rover."

Two incidents in the first week of medical school convinced me that I was either going to laugh a lot or cry a lot. My first "exposure" to medical school was our entry physical. I stood in a long shivering line, stripped to my shorts, awaiting my turn to be examined. My main concern was wondering if that cold looking stethescope-bedecked intern was going to smile and say, "You're okay." Needless to say, he didn't and he and I soon engaged in a one-sided sparring match. After sternly telling me to relax he proceeded to poke, pull, pry and pulverize every crease and orifice that I had once considered mine, with not so much as a grunt or nod of approval. All I heard was what I thought was "shoddy nose" and "next." I rapidly pulled my shorts back in place and bounced to my clothes heap. I was confused and worried. He had his index finger buried in my groin when he grunted "shoddy nose" to the intern filling out the forms. My nose may be odd and his knobby index finger was long indeed, but how could he belittle my nose with his finger in my groin?

Two years later I heard a professor describe a patient's lymph nodes as "shotty," meaning like small shot or pebbles. That's about what we all have but why did I have to wait so long to find out that I didn't need a nose transplant?

One day after my physical exam I got my second jolt at our first anatomy lecture. "Good morning, *boys,* welcome to medical school. I would like to tell you that one-fourth of you won't be here after the first anatomy exam. Of those of you who do pass, one or two of you will die of cancer of the testicle before or after you graduate." Now I was confused. I didn't know what to check first on my daily physical that we all began giving ourselves. My nose was concern enough; thank goodness I didn't have a full length mirror!

As we progressed with our medical training, we began to see regular patients in the hospital clinic. This was much like the setting of a doctor's office, as patients with minor problems came and went. One day a lady came in with what we suspected was a liver disease, and she was instructed to collect a 24-hour stool specimen and take it to the laboratory for analysis. About three weeks later I received a call from the laboratory, with a *very* disgruntled lab technician on the other end. She snarled:

"I wish you 'doctors' would please give more specific instructions to your patients. There's a lady here with a wagon full of – – – –. (The technician meant to say 'stool,' I'm sure.) She's got boxes and jars full of it, and says she was told to bring in a 24-*day* collection." The hot August days had not helped "preserve" the "specimen."

"Laughter is the best medicine," the saying goes. How does it work? It's a two-way street, and works best when a patient stands his ground and hands it right back to me. Then it helps us both. Patient's invariably do.

One of my more cantankerous older ladies came in one day and had her usual edge on. She had wanted to die for years and had always asked me for something to expedite it. She was very serious about it. I had always refused on the grounds that she should pay her taxes as well as I and I would not let her off the hook. She usually accepted it with a snort of contempt and went on to her other troubles. One day she brought in a stack of clippings from the newspaper, all "doctor tell me" columns and thrust them at me.

"Read these," she said. "Is that what's wrong with me?"

I pulled in a deeper breath than usual and thumbed through them in despair.

"Don't look disgusted at me, doctor. If you damned doctors would talk to us, the newspaper doctors wouldn't have a job." I broke down laughing and she managed a small triumphant smile.

The hospital will never forget the lady who came in one night with a sheet wrapped around her walking in a most unladylike fashion. After reaching the relative privacy of the emergency room, she began to remove the sheet, hesitantly. She said:

"It's so terrible and I'm so ashamed. You've never seen anything like this before. I'm not sure I should even show you."

By now the duty intern and the nurses were fully awake, and they tried to reasssure her that, whatever it was, they would understand. They asked her to please remove the sheet.

"Oh, I'm just mortified," the woman continued. "My husband varnished the toilet seat and didn't tell me. And I'm stuck to it!"

She then dropped the sheet, displaying a shiny toilet seat firmly attached to her ample rear. Well, nurses and doctors (even interns) are supposed to be somewhat professional, but this scene destroyed any remnant of professionalism. The intern took one unbelieving look, rocked back in laughter and said:

"My God, I've seen them every way but framed!"

The intern AND the patient were weak with laughter two hours later when careful use of a solvent and frequent washing successfully brought removal of the "frame."

Tragedy or comedy?

One Sunday morning while Carolyn and I were having breakfast the telephone rang. An old fellow with a shaky voice was hollering into the phone. "Say," he said, "I was fishing yesterday and now I'm all swollen with poison oak." I really didn't need to ask "where" because fishermen only get poison oak in one place, but I did.

"Where is it, John?" I asked.

"It's my privates, where else?" he thundered. "It's swollen and it itches like hell — I need help bad."

"Well, tell me where you shop and I'll call something out," I said.

"What are you going to give me," he asked.

"Some medicine, something to take the swelling and itching

out," I reassured him. He was talking to his wife at the same time and the conversation became quite disjointed.

"What's that, something to do what, well just a minute," he would say, and I could hear his wife hollering in the background again.

Then he would yell to his wife, "He says it's something to get rid of the swelling and itching. He's going to call me out some medicine." Then she would holler something back. He finally said, "Just a minute, doctor," and put the phone down for what seemed like an eternity. He came back and asked, "Well, what is it you're going to call out?"

My egg was getting cold and I was getting hot. I couldn't understand what was going on between them. Finally, in desperation, I asked, "What's the problem, John? Do you want to know the chemical name or what? It's an antihistamine and is very safe."

He said, "Just a minute" again and put the phone back down once more. I heard a distant barrage between him and his wife. Finally he returned and said, "Well say, change the medicine will you? Call out something that will remove this itching but leave the swelling."

Tragic problems don't warrant a tragic face as the psychiatrist implied. The more tragic the problem the less we can afford the long sad face and the more we need a cheery note.

A 64-year-old man came in with chest pains. He was having obvious angina and an electrocardiogram revealed an early heart attack. I gave him a shot of morphine and called an ambulance. He was upset and said, "You know, doctor, today is my 40th wedding anniversary."

I knew him and his family very well and had cared for them for many years. I said, "Well, after living with that gal for 40 years it's no wonder! Probably quite fitting that it happened today."

He mustered a chuckle and said, "You're sure right, I just hadn't thought of it that way."

He was taken to the hospital and placed in the Intensive Care Unit. He died later that night. Several weeks later his wife came in to thank me for his care and what had been done for him.

"I was so upset to see him in Intensive Care with all the gadgets hooked up to him. I really thought I wasn't going to make it, it was such a shock. Just before he died he pulled me down and with a big grin whispered what you and he had said in the office. That did it, that got me through it. I knew I would make it after that. It's the only thing that got me through the night and the funeral. Everytime things got too bad, I just thought about that comment and it pulled me through. It was much better than any tranquilizer I could have taken!"

Why does laughter help? Why is it "such good medicine?" It's an emotion. We know that 75 percent of our illnesses are caused

134

by our emotions. If the emotions of anxiety, depression and despair that we're packing around from marital discord and job-related stress are the source of our health problems, it only follows that a different set of emotions might have a beneficial effect. I think that's why a light-hearted approach — the twinkle in our eye or the ability to laugh — is so beneficial. And when we think about it, we really only have the one choice to make. Are we going to carry the world on our shoulders and pay with our health or bounce along and give ourselves a break? We can't afford to take what I call the "manhole" view of the world.

Doctors need to remind themselves of this more than anyone. We are constantly dealing with sick and unfortunate people. It's contagious if you don't get your guard up. One associate calls it the "doctor disease" or the "gray disease." Wearing a feeling of gloom and doom. Doctors are taught early in training that if you don't push yourself to the limit and beyond you're a failure by definition. Consequently, we pay a high price with coronaries, divorce, suicide, drug addiction and alcoholism. It doesn't have to be this way. When I'm sick I want a doctor who isn't pushed beyond his limits, who doesn't have the "gray disease," and who can tell me my problems without a look of despair. I'd like some "good news" with the "bad news" even if he has to look to find it.

Being on the receiving end of the joke has made many a day for me. A lady brought in an eight-week-old girl for her routine checkup. I had not seen the family nor the baby before and after examining the infant it was obvious that she was somewhat undernourished and was not gaining weight properly. I asked if the baby was breast fed or bottle fed. "Breast fed," she replied. After examining the infant I asked her if she would get in a gown so I could examine her breasts and left the room for a minute. She seemed puzzled as I scurried out the door. I returned and after a brief examination, I said, "No wonder the baby's not gaining weight. You shouldn't be nursing at all. Your breasts are completely dry."

"Oh, I'm not," she smiled. "The mother takes care of that. I'm just the babysitter." Maybe being the butt of dumb doctor jokes should hurt, but it "busted" both of us up.

One thing I have noticed is that the stronger I build my defensive wall, the more I can count on someone tunneling under. Fred Harkins, a pharmaceutical representative, who has called on me for years, is a continual pebble in my boot.

I have a sailfish mounted on my office wall. This has apparently troubled Fred for some time. One day in a more demeaning manner than usual he inquired, "Why is it that you and so many other doctors have large fish or animal trophies hanging so inconspicuously on your walls?"

This was *my* moment. I pulled myself up in what I

considered my most professional stance and said, seriously, "I'm glad you asked. That's the way we learn. I can't speak for the others, but I have mine on the wall for the obvious reason — to remove once and for all any doubt about my manhood in the eyes of my patients and the world!"

He grimaced slightly. "I see," he said.

"That should prove enough for the patients and the world," he offered. "Now how about yourself?"

It's true "he who laughs, lasts." Look at your friends and acquaintances. Why are some so much fun to be around and why do others brighten up a room by walking out? I'm convinced we all have a sense of humor tucked away somewhere. If you haven't been using yours, dust it off and put it in the medicine chest. Try it first the next time there's "nothing to bandage." It has a broad range and plays no favorites. It's the only medicine I know that works equally well for ulcers, headaches, fatigue, colitis and the rest of our self-inflicted ailments. Humor can rapidly diminish the distance we tend to place between ourselves and those around us. This is the first step and the reverse is also true: the more distance put between us the less humor we use. Let's look at an example. Two people run into each other going around the corner in the hall. What happens?

"Excuse me, I'm sorry, it's my fault" — always said with a smile.

"No, it's my fault. I should have been looking. Just call me Grace."

"Care to dance," chuckle, etc.

Now let's wrap a piece of metal around each of us in the form of an automobile and see what happens at the intersection when someone tries to sneak into the lane of traffic after waiting ten minutes. All cars immediately form a bumper to bumper wedge, and if the poor soul does sneak in, windows are rolled down, fists waved and a cloud of blue profanity goes up that would put a pollution detector out of order. No "care to dance" or "my fault" stuff here. No one's laughing. We've got a little distance between us. It's a distance our health can't afford.

And a Christmas card from a twelve-year-old girl will always be special to me;

"Dear Dr. Fisher — I haven't seen you for awhile because you keep me so well. When I do come in sick you always tell me something funny and I forget I'm sick. You've got a good thing going, your friend and patient, Cindy."

And, a Christmas letter from the Far East convinces me that the humor chapter *was* necessary:

Dear Doctor Fisher:

I do not expect you to remember me, but I still want to send you a note of thanks for taking such good care of my parents.

136

We understand they played hookey from you for a couple of years, even though they were telling us that they saw you faithfully every six months.

My sister finally got them back in to see you, and it is a very big relief for all of us.

Thank you not only for the medical care you have provided my parents, but most of all for being able to handle them and get them to do the things they should. I think Mom loves to see you because she knows you may scold her, but also will tease her (and no woman is too old for that!).

Thanks again, not only from my husband and myself, but please know the family is very appreciative. Merry Christmas to you and your staff.

I am convinced no woman, or no man, is ever too old or too young to be teased.

11 – Before We Go

We've covered a lot of ground about you and me. I stepped on a few toes, I hope, including my own. We don't usually jump into action unless we feel a need, and that's really what I've tried to do: to put enough pressure on all of our toes to make us pull them back and think. If we can do this, it may be a new day dawning. We're going to have to do something if we're going to keep body and soul intact.

I can't tell you how to repair a damaged ego, or how to make the elderly middle-aged, the middle-aged youthful, regain lost confidence, open the door to new careers or re-ignite the flame of romance. I'll have to leave that to the "hair restorers" who write ads.

The terrain we've been through has not been the valley of paradise. I haven't intended it as such for in honesty, it couldn't be. Nor is it the valley of despair. I prefer to call it the valley of hope. We've seen some beautiful meadows and some boulder-strewn paths. I hope I've led us all to a few "detour" signs, to have us consider possible alternate routes in our unending search for health and happiness.

I haven't asked you to wear your "positive mental attitude" buttons that we see at so many of the sales meetings. An attitude is not something you can pin on. It has to blossom from inside. The trouble with trying to pin on a positive mental attitude is that you lose it when you walk in the door and throw your coat in the big chair, and this may be when you need it most. I haven't given you a two week program of things to do to "get it all together," no "Fifteen Easy Steps to a New You." We've all seen enough of those. I'm reminded of a gal in her late twenties who had several of the latest "get it together" books in her hand at a bookstore. As she was walking toward the cash register, she turned to a friend and, in a loud voice, said: "Fantastic! I'll be a new me before I get home." Any bets?

All I'm really asking is that you stop, look, talk, listen and maybe laugh. That's a big enough request! The rewards will be just as big.

I've left some loose ends, I know. A lot of new ground has been broken. I have tried to plow under some old barren ground, namely that of typing and labeling people. A good many studies have been done trying to equate one personality type with a certain illness. I've tried to avoid this approach. It's the "typing stuff" that we're better off without! Doctors were taught years ago that we could probably diagnose what illness a patient had by a mere "psychological analysis." The patient was interviewed but no symptoms were mentioned. It didn't really work out and I don't think we can wrap things up so neatly. Human beings are too complex. We've shown that all of us can alter our uncontrollable nervous system in about any way we like, or don't like. It seems fruitless to me to start trying to draw equations.

To say that these thoughts and behavior equals arthritis, or that these emotions equal ulcers or migraine headaches, just doesn't hold up under the spotlight. I think the reason is quite obvious. If we're going to have a chemical reaction (or a physical equation), we often need a catalyst to get it going. We at least have to mix the chemicals together. This is where we stumble in our "real life" equation. Too many things in our life change, including the weather. In other words, if we use a different catalyst each time, or put in a slightly different amount of chemicals, our equation will change by definition. We're changing all the time both physically and mentally whether we accept it or not. Our outlook on life and our response to the world around us are in a continual state of change. An event that might lead to an ulcer this year may be totally ineffective five years from now, depending on how we change or don't change. The opposite is also true. An event that may only roughen up our stomach lining a bit with a diagnosis of nervous indigestion, may result in three bleeding ulcers and a gastric resection two years later. This is why the character typing doesn't get us very far. We're not really interested in getting typed, we're interested in getting well. We may be the "type" who has learned to override one portion of our uncontrollable nervous system to perfection but we can also "branch out" into other body systems later, or at the same time. Most likely we will attempt to override several body systems and end up with several symptoms, not just one.

This is what happens in my practice when I goof up and merely treat symptoms. I can fool myself and the patient (maybe) but I can't fool the patient's body. If I don't look beyond the obvious and realize that something is behind the ulcer, we're going to get the results I deserve. Treatment of the ulcer or nervous stomach goes along well, then out pops another set of symptoms. The body isn't going to settle for any patched-up affair. It's unhappy with this character that's carrying it around and its warning lights are flashing on the control panel that we talked about. If we numb this portion of the body with medication and don't change our approach, the nervous system has a board meeting and plans an attack in another portion of the body.

It's like the time I tried to patch 200 feet of cheap plastic hose that had been lying in the 90 degree heat at our little acreage. (It had been on sale for a reason, I found out, but the price was right.) I would patch one spot and turn on the pressure. Then another spot, several feet away, would start to spray. I had run over the hose with the tractor several times and assumed that I had nicked it in several places. After returning to the tool box for plastic tape and turning off the pressure several times, I finally got the message. Once I began to look closely I could see a small blister slowly begin to form when I turned the water on. The blister rapidly blossomed and finally ruptured leaving a small geyser. It was obvious, even to me, the hose was worthless and wouldn't take the pressure. How many times do you and I do that to ourselves? With a cheap plastic hose problem, I got the message on the fourth geyser. With our bodies and health, we're usually quite different. We tend to stand in the geyser and wonder why so much rain has to fall into our life!

As one 36-year-old patient told me early in my practice, "You'll be seeing lots of me. I never get over one problem completely before something else begins. It's kinda crazy really. It's almost as though my body's fighting me."

His body was fighting him and, unfortunately, the body was winning — or losing.

It has taken me so long to grasp the most obvious and important secret to your and my well-being. It's now so graphically clear that I really do it an injustice to call it a secret. A loud speaker has been screaming it at me for years. The "secret" is this. Most of our illnesses are merely the beginning of the healing process. Please read that statement again. It's one of the most important points I have to make. Stop for a few minutes and think it over. How I missed the message so long I'll never know, but it sailed right by me and most of my colleagues. Be honest with yourself; you've probably missed it too. Remember the odds we mentioned before. You and I are the ones responsible for most of our illnesses. Or, as the patient said, it is as if our bodies are fighting us. We're looking at it wrong, though. Our bodies are fighting *for* us, not *against* us. I see so many patients who complain:

"Why am I so tired? Why do I have one health problem after another? What's wrong with me, anyway?"

I have to point out that they are not seeing the picture clearly. The facts actually are turned around: they should be standing in amazement at the amount of stress and tension their body has taken. The body has been a marvel, not a failure. But the body can only take so much; it's "only human." When the body has had enough, we begin to get subtle warnings, such as an occasional headache, fatigue, or abdominal cramps. This is the early warning system telling us that an illness is brewing, if we don't alter course or change our daily patterns. These early symptoms are really the body's way of saying: "Help, let's turn things around. Let's stop this destructive pattern and begin repairs." This is the beginning of the healing process. This is what

140

makes the illness only the beginning of health if we will pay attention to it.

The body is literally saying, "Look, we've got a problem. I can't pack you around in your condition any longer. You're placing unrealistic demands on yourself and all of the 'gang' inside, and we can't take it. You're overriding every judgment the autonomic nervous system sends me and things are in a mess inside. The only way I know to get your attention is to send some smoke signals and here they are. Can you feel the palpitations or heart pounding? How about the headache; that must hurt! Are those mean old stomach cramps and burning getting to you? How about the fatigue, doesn't it make my point; and the diarrhea, I'll bet you can't ignore that even if you tried?"

I've got news for our aching bodies. You and I can ignore all the "smoke" until we've either asphyxiated from it or our skeletal house burns down. We're experts at ignoring such things. If we seek help, someone usually helps us neatly arrange the smoke signals with their "skywriting" ability:

"Here are the medications you need to be able to live with a "fire" inside, tranquilizers, pain killers and anti-spasmodics."

This is where the medical profession has got to take a new approach. We can't afford to get lost in laboratory tests, X-rays, medications and the latest technological achievements. It's a dangerous one-way road. We can't head out the door for a three-day seminar on fire fighting techniques with smoke pouring out of the basement. We've got to see the obvious, the results of stress at work. It won't matter what's new in fire extinguishers. By the time we get back we won't need them. The early warning set of symptoms may now have raged into a serious illness. If we do find the source, we can't just "put it out." We've got to find out what caused it and make the necessary corrections.

Tranquilizers, pain killers and anti-spasmodics are great. They have a place and we can all be thankful for them. I don't want a congressional committee deciding when you and I can have one as we're now beginning to feel. The more of this I see, the more tranquilizers I'm going to need! As I mentioned earlier, the committees are worrying in the wrong directions anyway. They would do well to worry about the reasons for the use of these drugs rather than the quantity being used. The government's inconsistencies are showing. If I can buy all the government controlled and taxed alcohol and tobacco that I need for the next 50 years without a prescription, I'd like to think that I can get a sedative or an effective cough syrup without an act of Congress. It's only fair even if they're not taxed.

I want us to have a "crutch" when we need it. Crutches are great and I spell this out to patients before they nail me with, "Isn't that a crutch?" If they don't want a crutch, they're in the wrong place. That's my business, a crutch shop, and that's just what I call it. Crutches and fire extinguishers both have a place. We have to start by putting out the fire and smoke. We need all the help we can get. We have to reconsider the terrible term "crutch." What's so bad about it? To me it's a support, a real help. Most patients with a broken leg leave my office with one. I've yet to see a patient who felt he was a "lesser person" because he needed one to walk with. The same goes for the other problems. If a tranquilizer or anti-spasmodic for the stomach or bowel can help us, we should use them. I couldn't practice at home or in the office without them. Let's use them like we would any good crutch, to support us *while* we're getting better. We can't forget that a crutch is a temporary help. It's like the fire extinguisher and just as important. Tranquilizers can be a great help to us all. I think it's good medicine to "cool" the control panel if every flashing bulb is lit and overheating. This is no time to light up one more bulb with more symptoms that result from an attitude of "not me, I don't want it, no crutches, please." I call it a medical vacation and that's not all bad. One month on the French Riviera might possibly do the same thing, but there may be a few dollars and miles between us and the French Riviera. A medical vacation may be the best that you and I can do for the time being.

Sedatives or tranquilizers tend to calm us and we usually feel better. Herein lies part of the help. If we lose most of the symptoms and feel "so much better" on a medication that merely reduces our tension and stress, or our interpretation of it, we should have learned something. This shows us "how good" we could feel and should feel if we give ourselves a chance. We may need it pointed out, but usually my patients see it without my coaching. They may be a little surprised. "I can't believe it, I just didn't think nerves could do all that."

One 35-year-old man who had asthma to a life-threatening degree came in short of breath and gasping for air. He required cortisone and adrenalin injections and got rapid relief. He had been everywhere and was on all the right medications. He had been on allergy shots for 7 years. After seeing him on three occasions in 10 days, we had to do something differently. I stopped all of his medication and added a new one, a rather strong tranquilizer. He didn't keep his next appointment but called me on the phone.

He said, "I can't believe it, I just can't, after all this time. I've never felt better, I haven't had a single wheeze. I've stopped coughing up all the phlegm. How did you know?" Simply from listening to him tell me how "smooth" his life was and that tension was not a factor. After all, a long series of "courtroom battles" over the children would soon be over and the family feuding would end. He got the message; we stopped the sedation

142

and he calls now and then to let me know "it's still hard to believe."

When we talk about crutches, *temporary* is the key word. If the crutch isn't temporary, problems arise. I know of no vacation, medical or actual, where we can play now and pay later forever. We'll get in a bind if we prolong the play and postpone the pay too long. It sounds great and is a little tempting to take the easy road, just stay on the tranquilizers forever and forget paying the price of making some changes. When this happens, the crutch has grown to the cast and creates a problem all its own. We will all, no doubt, need a crutch of some sort in our lifetime, no one is immune.

An authority on stress and related illnesses, I once heard speak, tends to bear this out. His enlightening talk to 500 physicians told how to do a better job of handling stress. He ended his talk with, "I enjoyed being with you, you've been a swell audience. I've tried to show you the work we've done and the results of our studies. We feel we've shown a direct correlation between life stresses and illnesses. I have proved it to myself again today by coming before this large group. I started the day with diarrhea and I will end it with a migraine headache." I hope he used a crutch.

That physician may be ahead of most of us. He at least has his problems out in the open, and is admitting his stress to 500 doctors (not that they could help him)! Most of us have trouble admitting the presence of stress and tension even to ourselves. WE'RE above that sort of thing. One of my patients, a successul businessman, is completely blinded by the facts when he says:

"I don't understand. The more business I have, the more money I make, and the worse I feel."

I see many patients who are willing to work on their stress problem in order to start the healing process, but who feel like a failure if their symptoms reoccur. We seem to feel we have to conquer an illness once and for all. We feel we're hopeless if we have a relapse and get back in our old rut.

This tends to defeat us and it really shouldn't. We may never get "cured" but we can sure get a lot better. Just getting better, or showing improvement will help us realize we are on the right trail. Some of us have longer trails to walk than others. A 25 percent improvement may be more work for you and me than a 100 percent cure for our friends. It should be just as much, if not more, rewarding. I see people who have done so much for themselves that it's truly remarkable. They've come a long way, yet they may still feel like a loser. One 47-year-old lady has had some real crosses to bear. She has two handicapped children with little family support. She's made some long and painful strides at self-improvement and has obtained some nice results. Yet she feels like a loser.

She tells me, "I want a book for losers. Dr. Malz and Dr. Lair aren't losers. You aren't a loser yourself, you're all winners. I need a book by a loser that understand what it's like down here." She's truly searching for a book for losers. She had better reconsider the evidence. If Dr. Maltz and Dr. Lair had been winning, they would not have needed their books. Dr. Maltz wrote his book because his plastic surgery was not getting the results he expected. He could only give his patients a new face, not a new attitude. Jess Lair wrote his because his old "winning ways" weren't working. I've written mine because I am not getting people well. I'm not able to take any new patients, because I just don't have the time. I used to think that was a status symbol, but now I see it for what it really is. I can't take new patients because I can't get my "old ones" well. So, I think that lady's approach was wrong, even if she sees us as "winners." She wants to become a winner, not a loser. If you have tuberculosis, you're better off getting care from someone who knows how to treat it, rather than someone who has it.

I hope I haven't made this self-healing process look clear-cut and easy. It isn't. But recognizing symptoms and trying to remove the stress is where it has to start. And, I don't have all the answers, I'm still asking questions. Medical research and all of our scientists are not to be put down. You and I probably owe our lives to their efforts. It's not a matter of being for or against one approach. We can't afford separate "this" or "that" camps. I want all of the camp tools in the same tent. As Dr. Meier Friedman, co-author of *TYPE A BEHAVIOR AND YOUR HEART* told me, "I'm for everything that will help; we can't afford less." That.s why he and Dr. Rosenmann wrote their book. To add something, not to detract.

We talked about three patients of mine with Multiple Sclerosis. They all feel strongly they can relate to an emotional crisis that preceeded it. This doesn't mean a crisis caused their illness. I suggested earlier than an emotional upheaval and personality disruption may well be a causative factor. It would be a cruel injustice to everyone with Multiple Sclerosis or any other serious medical affliction of unknown cause, to stop here. We aren't going to.

Excellent research is now in progress that suggests a viral cause or etiology — for Multiple Sclerosis. Is this a matter of who's right or wrong? No! We're still looking for answers for a host of serious disabling diseases such as cancer, Hodgkin's disease, rheumatoid arthritis, ulcerative colitis, degenerative muscle and nerve disorders.

Doctors should all be looking closely together at the problems — not at each other. We've got to keep the doors wide open — all the way.

If we do find a virus responsible for this or that affliction, we're still not done. We're just beginning. Why doesn't everyone get these problems? If it's a virus, why isn't it more contagious? Why don't these diseases spread in epidemic form? Or do they in a slower fashion? Or could we all be "right?" Could it be that we weaken ourselves with physical and emotional drains to the point that these viral agents simply come marching in unopposed? Or does the virus lie dormant in all of us, just waiting for us to lower our immune defensive weapon?

I am a chronic victim of the cold sore, or herpes simplex in medical terms. There seems little doubt in medical circles that the cause for herpes is a virus. That's probably how it got the "cold" sore label. My repeated herpes of the lips have made me a little suspicious. I get one every eight to twelve months, yet I haven't had a sniffle in three years. I now have my herpes pretty well timed. Mine start to sting a little, and then an early swelling starts 24 to 30 hours after a stressful situation. These stress situations aren't all that earth-shaking: perhaps a difficult case in the hospital, a problem at the office, or a deadline to finish a manuscript. My last herpes came after a mad two days trying to figure out how to wash my clothes, get all the plants watered, and clear a path into the house just before Carolyn came back from a three-week stay with her mother who had undergone surgery. For those of you who get these miserable lip blisters, do a little research on your own. Go back a few days and see if anything had you as disturbed as I was with my housekeeping.

We accept the viral theory with the lesser illnesses such as colds, flu and infectious mononucleosis. As one mother whose son was in the hospital with infectious mononucleosis told me, "I knew Paul was going to come down with mono. We told him so. You see, he's working two long jobs." No questions asked about what caused it, what tests can we do — is it viral or tension induced. Mother tells me!

A professor in medical school nearly brought the roof down one day. He lectured about emotions and illnesses for a solid hour. It was the only hour spent on such a frivolous topic during the four years of medical school. He finished the lecture with, "We must consider emotion as a factor in all illnesses. I know of none in which emotions may not be a major causative factor. I'm not so sure but what emotions may even be at the basis of cancer."

The entire class erupted in thunderous laughter. He paused and probably expected the response. After we settled down and quit poking each other in the ribs he added a sobering thought that brought few laughs as we filed out. He said; "Laugh if you will but let us remind ourselves what cancer is — it's a cell gone mad."

How does a cell go mad? We don't know, despite a mountain of research. It is true, though, cancer is a cell gone wild — a cell that is multiplying without direction of any type in a progressive and deadly manner. The professor may have been ahead of his time, for medical journals rapidly are beginning to consider the questions, "Is cancer linked to personality traits?" and "Is life style related to cancer?"

Evidence linking cancer and emotions is being reported. The Third International Symposium on Detection and Prevention of Cancer reported that researchers in England and America have reached similar conclusions about breast cancer in women, namely that women who rigidly suppress their emotions, as well as those who strongly vent their feelings, are likelier candidates for cancer than women who go through life with more moderate emotions. This information sent me digging through my own files, and I was shocked when I reviewed the cases of breast cancer that I had detected. Nearly all of the women had had one of our top ten major life upheavals within two years of the cancer being detected. One of the exceptions was a lady who was seriously concerned about her husband's declining health. The other exception was one who had seen the life savings that she and her husband had accumulated vaporize in a disastrous investment over an 18-month period. Nearly every other woman was either in the midst of an impending or actual divorce or in a prolonged period of sharp marital discord.

We can't say that emotions cause cancer, but neither should we turn our heads in disbelief.

We're using the term "auto-immune" more and more to categorize a host of illnesses. What does it mean? Simply stated, auto- or self-immunized or protected. We have temporarily placed numerous illnesses in this auto-immune disease category.

We should really call these "lack of auto-immunity" diseases. The implication is the same. The body has somehow produced a reactivity to its own tissues as a result of an altered immunological response. That's a long way to say it. I think the patient summed it up best when he said, "I think my body's fighting me." The net result is that somehow our self protection gets lost.

There is much debate going on attempting to find the right category for numerous illnesses. As our colon authority put it "is it infectious, auto-immune or psychological?" Then he wanted to toss out psychological factors for us because it wasn't practical. We can't toss it out. To me it makes more sense to throw it right in the center of the ring — to make emotions the very core of the entire problem. Then we can begin to fit some loose pieces together.

If our emotions are this important and are given their proper respect for our well-being, it's possible to see how a major emotional upheaval can lead to all the rest. We can then alter our auto-immunity — or our self-defenses. Technically said, we can "produce a reactivity to our own tissues." At this point it's just possible that the viral and infectious diseases, the auto-immune diseases and a host of others might consider us an easy target. Personally, I'm going to try to keep my emotional upheavals to a minimum.

I had one 19-year-old boy who was totally upset with being inducted into the military service. He came to me to see if any of his past or present health problems could possibly prevent him from being inducted. The current examination and laboratory studies were normal, and his past medical history was not of any consequence to the military. He was thoroughly distraught. He came back a few weeks later with a new problem. He was beginning to lose weight and was unable to eat. He was weak and began to bruise easily. I was concerned. He looked quite pale and I repeated his blood count. It strongly suggested leukemia. A bone marrow study was done and examined by three different pathologists in two different hospitals and at the medical school. All were positive — it was acute lymphocytic leukemia. I wrote a letter to the draft board advising them of his condition and he was deferred. He shortly began to improve and no treatment had been instituted. I followed him closely and he continued to gain weight and improve. His blood count continued to improve and all subsequent bone marrow studies were normal. He recovered completely and remains healthy today!

If we can see the hazards of failing to control our stress, we're in a better position. I know I drive the most dangerous section of freeway in the state of Oregon twice a day. That's a real help to me. I watch it all the way, but it doesn't upset me. It's back to acceptance. If I accept the unpleasant fact that it's a wild stretch, I can change to correct for it if I need to. I can slow down, leave lots of room between me and the rest and not write myself notes as I've been known to do elsewhere. I can steer with both hands and not drive with my knees while I light my pipe.

It's the same with life. Once you and I accept the "secret" that I was so slow to see — that every illness is the body's attempt to get us back on our trail to health — we've got a better chance. We can change our ways or change roads. We can't stay on the same old road if we're having one collision after another. We have to change our approach — or try a different road.

We've got to do a better job of accepting our friends and family as they are. If we start looking for imperfections, we'll find many to dwell upon. Most of us are guilty of this in varying degrees, tending to accept others in limited portions at limited times. It won't work, and you and I have pretty well proved it. We seem so slow to accept the good fortunes of our friends but lend an attentive ear to any of their misfortunes.

We can't let someone or something wreck our day. Actually, no one else really wrecks a day for us — we "select" a person, a comment or an event that has riled us up and proceed to let the day become an emotional disaster all on our own, because we figure we're entitled to it. But we're the one who loses in situations like this.

We can't spend many days with an "I'll show them" attitude. It's too heavy a load. We can't put our bright lights on to blind them even if they forget to dim theirs. That makes the road more stressful and hazardous. It's bad enough to have one driver blinded as we pass each other along the way. Put both of our "brights" on and we're both blinded. It's impossible to see the middle of the road in this condition.

I go fishing with a dedicated river guide on occasions. I'm a "bonus" fisherman. I love the day in the boat or on the bank. If I catch fish, that's a bonus. It's not the way I'd like it, but with my skill it's a good philosophy to have. After one long day of fishing and not a single strike, the guide didn't seem to want to stop. He obviously wanted a fish. I told him the day was a total treat and I couldn't have had more fun. It was almost a true statement. I asked him if most of his customers put the pressure on him to "catch fish or else."

The guide summed it up so well for all of us, "No, no, not really," he said. "I can't ever remember one pressing me, but then they really don't need to — I do that to myself." That's us — you and me. That's the stuff we've got to work on. We can't put it on ourselves and we shouldn't put it on others.

We've got to stop what I call the "teeter-totter syndrome." We developed the idea early on the playground when we bounced on the teeter-totter. When we put someone down we automatically went up. What we tend to forget is the terrible jolt we got at the top, if we sent the one on the other end down too fast.

As one of my manuscript assistants said, "Why do we all work so hard at making everyone feel quivery inside." I like that. It couldn't be said better.

We've got to start giving of ourselves even if it's not "deductible." Deductible giving isn't giving anyway. To deduct is to subtract — that's what we're doing in our hearts. It's "getting" two for the price of one — a good feeling and a tax break. That's us again — giving with a purpose. That's me and the piano lessons. We're all guilty.

We've done so much for "them" and they have never returned the favor. We're telling on ourselves. We weren't really giving — we were expecting something! It's back to setting up franchises.

One short scene will stay with me the rest of my life. I was driving through downtown Portland in the urban renewal and new highrise apartment area. As I stopped for a red light I saw a mother in her late 20s with two screaming children. She had waist length straight hair and a velvet skirt with a revealing slit in it. The girl was about 8 and the boy about 6. The girl was sobbing hard but the little guy was screaming hysterically, "Mommy, let's go back, please, please, let's go back." The children had large paper sacks with what appeared to be their life's possessions with clothes and tennis shoes sticking out on top. The little boy had a clear plastic folder with his tablets, books and colors in it. Papers began to fall out in the pouring rain as he sobbingly tugged at his mother's skirt in total hysteria. He would try to reach down and grab a few soggy papers and invariably lose more as he did. The mother was watching traffic with a large smile and a careful eye. She was twisting about with her twirling skirt gaping. She obviously wanted a ride but had to settle things down a bit first.

"Help me, Mommy," the little boy screamed pathetically with his clothes and school supplies falling into the water.

"Okay," I heard her yell, and then watched in total horror. She grabbed his sack of clothes, his precious little plastic binder — lifted them high over her head and threw them crashing out into the busy wet street. The little guy, more hysterical than ever, ran out with swollen blinded eyes and started grabbing what he could. My light had turned and cars were honking. As I slowly pulled away I looked up into the large truck with two fellows who had stopped for the opposite light. The little boy continued to grab what he could in front of the large truck. The truckers were laughing and trying to catch mother's eye along with the rest of her.

I had a lousy day — I didn't turn it around like I've asked you to do. I couldn't. The scene wrecked my day. I saw so much of what this book is all about in one short "stop light" capsule.

Here was a young mother and two children leaving something important — an apartment or room — and maybe someone. Those two children were more distraught than any I had ever seen. They were headed somewhere, at least mother was. I wondered for days what happened. Where they ended and what happened after that. I wondered about the chances for two children. When are they going to start rubbing society wrong and have to be "dealt with?" How will they find their Ground Zero or do they even have one? When will their stress illnesses begin to appear? How will we treat their hyperactivity syndrome? Would we want our children in the same schoolroom with such "undesirables?" Why don't they know right from wrong?

What's wrong with our schools? Why aren't these kids learning anything? Where did they learn such words? Why don't some kids care? It's society's free "spirit" attitude paying off. These are the early precincts reporting in.

I'm all for free spirits but broken spirits I can't take.

You and I are in the race together. We're both on the same track. We may have different starting positions, or be a few lengths ahead or behind one another, but we're all running together. We can't control the conditions of the track, but we can decide how we're going to run. We all spend the first half of the race trying to win the race or conquer the world. We spend the last half trying to conquer ourselves.

Robert Louis Stevenson said: "If your morals make you dreary, depend upon it. They are wrong." Likewise, if our running of the race makes us ill, we can depend upon it. We're running it wrong. In any case, may your hurting be less and less, and may all your bandages be small.

Dr. Donald Fisher may be contacted through The Touchstone Press, P.O. Box 81, Beaverton, Oregon 97005